baking
unplugged

baking UNPLUGGED

nicole rees

 JOHN WILEY & SONS, INC.

WILEY

For Janet Groft Kriner and Bill Buis

Published by John Wiley & Sons, Inc., Hoboken, New Jersey

Published simultaneously in Canada

For general information on our other products and services or for technical support, please
contact our Customer Care Department within the United States at (800) 762-2974, outside
the United States at (317) 572-3993 or fax (317) 572-4002.

Wiley also publishes its books in a variety of electronic formats. Some content that appears in
print may not be available in electronic books. For more information about Wiley products,
visit our web site at www.wiley.com.

LIBRARY OF CONGRESS CATALOGING-IN-PUBLICATION DATA

Rees, Nicole.
  Baking unplugged / by Nicole Rees.
    p. cm.
  Includes index.
  ISBN 978-0-470-14911-9 (cloth : all. paper)
1. Baking. I. Title.
  TX765.R38 2009
  641.8'15--dc22

        2008019013

FEB 1 2 2009

Designed by Debbie Glasserman

Printed in the United States of America
10 9 8 7 6 5 4 3 2 1

contents

acknowledgments

No creative endeavor is the result of a single mind. Without a world filled with talented chefs, writers, baking instructors, cooking experts, gifted friends, and gorgeous food magazines and newspaper articles, where would inspiration come from? And then there are the folks that help you along . . . I continue to be indebted to the fabulous editors at *Chocolatier Magazine*, *Fine Cooking*, and the *Oregonian's FoodDay*, where some of these recipes first appeared. My sincere gratitude goes also to my editor Pam Chirls, a true champion of bakers and chefs. And since I am much better at writing abbreviated (read: barely legible) recipes on sticky notes rather than fluid text, this book could not have been accomplished without the efforts of Lisa Bell, an editor and ex–pastry chef. Thank you, Lisa, for making space in your life for this obsession of mine.

introduction: the unplugged lifestyle

i am the misfit in my family, the only child to adore pastry and sweets so fervently that I expect one after every meal to this very day. My mother was not a baker. She would occasionally make cookies from scratch, but cakes, puddings, brownies, and muffins all started with a box. With supervision, I was allowed to bake from the age of eight. I was the one who climbed onto the counters to see what we had on hand for dessert. One day, there were no boxes, no mixes to be found. As I looked around the kitchen, waiting for inspiration to strike, I spotted an old, barely used copy of *The Joy of Cooking* and made a quick inventory of the kitchen. Flour, sugar, eggs, milk, vanilla, and baking powder . . . hmm, I would not go without dessert after all.

My love of desserts and my desire to learn the hows and whys of baking only increased over time. And I still bake just like I did when I was eight. That's the point of *Baking Unplugged.* Let me explain. Yes, my home and work kitchens are filled with modern gadgets. Yes, I have spent a number of very informative years working alongside PhDs, building the strongest possible foundation in food science. But like the television music show the title recalls, *Baking Unplugged* reveals how most of the recipes I really want to make at the end of the workday—simple, satisfying treats—require no special gadgets, skills, or ingredients, nor a lot of time. What I've learned is that a good grasp of basic proportions and some really simple fundamental techniques are what make for good baking.

I bake simple foods from scratch. I know from watching my mother that homemade is really no harder than futzing around with a mix. Mixes, after all, require added ingredients. And, more often than not, I leave the fancy mixer and food processor in the pantry and rely instead on a bowl and a whisk. Why should I listen to a whirring blender or mixer when I could be listening to my family or relaxing music?

Baking Unplugged is also my answer to people who've complained to me that baking is fussy: "Bakers are born, not made. . . . Baking is an art. . . . Baking is a science." Anyone can walk into the kitchen and bake something perfectly lovely without being genetically gifted or classically trained. That's what our grandmothers and great-grandmothers did, after all!

01.

THE UNPLUGGED KITCHEN

What I adore about baking is how little you need to get started. It seems I've had the same few bowls, spoons, and measuring cups for almost two decades. So in the face of gorgeous catalogs loaded with specialized equipment and ingredients, what is essential?

The Basics

ONE SET OF MEASURING SPOONS: Look for a set with deep wells. Some of the flimsy metal spoons have shallow wells that are hard to level, making accurate measuring difficult. Since you'll be measuring potent ingredients such as salt, baking soda, and yeast with these, you'll want to be as precise as possible.

ONE SET OF DRY MEASURING CUPS: Look for sturdy, straight-sided cups that are easy to level and have heavy-duty handles that don't easily bend. I have an extra-large set that includes a ⅔-cup and ¾-cup measure. You'll use these cups for measuring all dry ingredients, dried fruit, and even small amounts of frozen berries.

HEATPROOF GLASS (PYREX) LIQUID MEASURING CUPS: Have a good variety of these cups. I have 1-cup, 2-cup, 4-cup, and 8-cup measures. Sure, they're designed for measuring liquids, but the larger ones can also be used for mixing and pouring. I use the 8-cup for measuring fresh fruit for pies and for making simple batters and doughs.

Both liquid and dry measuring cups measure volume. Because they have different shapes, though, if you fill a 1-cup liquid measure and a 1-cup dry measure with flour, you will not have the same amount of flour by weight in each cup. It pays to use the right measuring tool for most dry ingredients, but especially for flour. Two tablespoons too much flour can make cakes or cookies tough and dry. Remember that 2 tablespoons of flour with 1 cup of liquid makes a thick gravy, so that's a lot of moisture-holding power! Milk will fit into the metal cups, of course, but without the markings on the clear glass liquid measure you can't make sure you've measured precisely.

BOWLS: You'll need at least three or four bowls ranging from 6" to 14" in diameter for mixing. Once upon a time, I had steel, ceramic, and glass bowls. Because the ceramic and glass bowls were so heavy, clunky, and breakable, I got rid of them. Now I only have lightweight, nonreactive stainless-steel bowls. I use the shallow bowls for tossing fruit and letting doughs rise, and for placing over a smaller pan of simmering water for a makeshift double boiler. Since metal conducts heat fast and does not suffer when exposed to temperature extremes, you can take a hot bowl and place it in an ice bath to rapidly cool a mixture down—custard, for example. I have a few bowls with high sides for whisking liquids together, beating egg whites, and whipping cream—much less splashing and sloshing that way.

KNIVES: There are only three essential knives you'll need, and you probably own all of them if you cook: a small paring knife, for splitting and scraping vanilla beans and other precise work; a 6" to 8" regular chef's knife, for chopping fruit, nuts, and chocolate; and a long serrated knife for neatly slicing breads and cakes.*

---

*I am not a knife snob. I own one expensive chef's knife. The rest are inexpensive and perfectly adequate.

SAUCEPANS: You'll need a small and medium saucepan for making custards, sauces, and fruit compotes. I have a heavy-duty stainless pan that heats evenly for making caramel. Sugar doesn't turn to caramel until you've exceeded 300°F, at which point a lesser pan reveals its shortcomings with hotspots. A stainless interior is best for judging color, too—essential for knowing when to remove the caramel from the heat. Also in my collection is a cheap, lightweight pan with a nonstick interior. I am not ordinarily a fan of nonstick pans, but I've found that I love to make quick skillet jams, fruit sauces, and preserves in this pan, because the nonstick surface cleans up so beautifully, and less fruit sticks to the side and burns.

BOX GRATER: You'll need a box grater for shredding zucchini and carrots for cakes (the largest holes—not the long slats for slicing) and for grating fresh ginger (use the smallest holes).

VEGETABLE PEELER: You'll need one of these for peeling apples and carrots. A vegetable peeler is the perfect tool for making lovely chocolate curls, too.

MICROPLANE ZESTER: These sharp, long tools make fast work of zesting, leaving you with a fluffy mass of flavorful fruit peel and no bitter pith.

A ROTARY (HAND-CRANKED) CHEESE GRATER: This ingenious little cheese grater is perfect for grinding nuts into a fine, light powder. The friction of grinding nuts in a food processor makes the nut meal oily and heavy—it's better for making nut butters.

WOODEN SPOONS: I keep my wooden spoons (along with silicone spatulas and whisks) in a ceramic pitcher right next to the stove top, so I can grab the one I want without having to open a drawer and dig around. In addition to regular wooden spoons, I have a flat-edged one whose greater surface area and sharper edge make creaming butter and sugar together more efficient.

SILICONE SPATULAS: Invest in a few heat-resistant silicone spatulas and you'll never regret it. The big ones are great for gently folding ingredients into batters, and the small ones help you get every last bit of melted chocolate, honey, or sour cream out of a measuring cup. Some spatulas have a slightly concave interior, making them perfect for spooning batters into pans. You can even use them in place of wooden spoons for stirring.

WHISKS: Whisks are my favorite kitchen tools. I use them for mixing dry ingredients together, which lightens and aerates them before they will be incorporated into a batter. If your flour or cocoa has no lumps, whisking can take the place of sifting.

I also use a whisk to combine the liquid ingredients—after I've whisked the dry, naturally, so I don't have to wash and dry the whisk. And since I often leave my butter sitting out near the stove where it gets meltingly soft, sometimes I use the whisk to cream the butter and sugar and then beat in the eggs in cake batters. I also whisk the oil, sugar, and eggs together for oil-based cakes. Whisks are, of course, essential in the unplugged kitchen for whipping cream and beating egg whites. If you have a teardrop-shaped balloon whisk with flexible loops that are well-spaced, you can also use it to begin the folding process, when you want to take care not to deflate eggs or cream as they are incorporated into a mousse.

I buy very inexpensive balloon whisks (as opposed to French whisks with their straighter shape and firmer metal loops), made of lightweight steel, that are easy to hold onto.

Look for thin, widely spaced, flexible loops—they will be gentler on batters and will whip cream faster. The lightweight metal will be easier on your arms, too, if you aren't used to whipping cream by hand.

JUICER: The reamer-style juicer is adequate, but for juicing any quantity of lemons, limes, or oranges, I like the traditional dome-style juicer with the juice reservoir at the bottom.

MESH STRAINERS OR SIEVES: I don't own a sifter; a mesh strainer is the best, handiest tool for me. Get at least two strainers—one fine-mesh screen and one regular. If I need to strain lumps from cocoa or brown sugar, I use a strainer. Ditto for a custard that has tiny lumps of overcooked egg in it. I also use them as colanders to wash berries. When a recipe calls for a small amount of coffee, I often mix the fine grounds directly in boiling water, let them steep for 5 minutes for maximum flavor, then sieve the coffee through a very fine-mesh strainer.

PARCHMENT PAPER: There is only one specialty item that I can't live without, and that's commercial parchment paper. You'll find this at restaurant- and cake decorating–supply stores. I buy a whole box of 1000 sheets at a time, which lasts for years, but many stores (or bakeries) will sell 10 or 20 sheets at a time. If you buy 18" x 12" rimmed baking sheets (aka half-sheet pans), half of a parchment sheet will fit the pan perfectly. Commercial parchment paper is much, much cheaper than the brown, waxy rolls of parchment sold in the supermarket. Plus, the rolled parchment constantly curls up at the edges and won't lie flat.

I bake cookies on parchment, which makes cleanup easy, slightly decreases how much the cookies spread, and moderates browning. I roll out cookie dough and pie pastry between sheets of parchment for ease. Parchment can also be rolled into cones to use for piping frosting or ganache.

ROLLING PIN: If you are heading out to the store, I vote for the straight rolling pin. At about 18" long, with a diameter of nearly 2", it is the most useful. I use it to crush cookies and flatten pie dough. Its long length makes rolling dough fast, easy, and precise.

OFFSET METAL SPATULAS: These look like very skinny spatulas with a bend in the blade toward the handle. The angle of the handle makes this little tool useful for inserting into tarts, pies, and baking pans to lift out a single serving of dessert. You'll need a large one and a small one. They're great for leveling off ingredients in dry measuring cups, smoothing out batters in pans, running around the edge of cake pans to loosen cakes, and spreading frostings and fillings on desserts.

A STAINLESS-STEEL (FIRM) OR A PLASTIC (FLEXIBLE) BENCH SCRAPER: When you're rolling out doughs or making bread, a bench scraper is your best friend. It loosens your dough when it sticks to the counter or wooden board, and it scrapes up every last bit of sticky dough on the rolling surface, thereby preventing more sticking. You'll also use it to divide dough into pieces or to scrape out a bowl. It's very handy.

PASTRY BLENDER: A pastry blender is the quick and easy way to cut fat into flour when making pie pastry, biscuits, or scones. You'll often see recipes that call for two knives to cut in the butter. I have to admit this has always baffled me, and I've never actually seen anyone do it. I personally would have more luck with two chopsticks. I fell in love with my grandmother's pastry blender when I was little, and I still think it's fun to mash the cold bits of butter and shortening with it.

COOKIE, BISCUIT, AND DOUGHNUT CUTTERS: You can go nuts with cookie cutters and end up with dozens for every occasion, but all you really need to get started is one 2½"- to 3"-round cutter for basic cookies, biscuits, and short-cakes. A doughnut cutter is really two round cutters nested together, so that you can go back and remove the ball of dough from the center of the dough-nut. Then, of course, you can fry up the doughnut holes, too.

BAKEWARE: Here's a basic list of the bakeware a home baker uses most. Don't feel pressured to go out and buy all these pans at once. You probably have a few of them, anyway, and it's best to let your food cravings dictate which pans to invest in next. Whether you buy entry-level pans at your local discount store or upgrade to name brands sold at department stores, the recipes will work regardless. On the facing page you'll see the kind of pans I used when preparing the recipes in this book, but with a small bake-time or temperature adjustment, bakeware of any material will do.

I prefer simple, light-colored metal pans to either heavy, dark metal pans or heatproof glass. Dark pans absorb heat easily and heavy pans absorb heat slowly due to their heft and so will brown delicate cakes and cookies more than light pans. While glass and ceramic pie plates make a prettier presentation, they are heavy and clunky to store—especially if you like to stash a bunch of pies in the freezer. Glassware does have the bonus of being clear, allowing you to gauge browning more easily—very appealing to a new baker. Glass is slower to heat in the oven and slower to cool down, and as a result, many books say it bakes "hotter" and to adjust the oven down 25 degrees when baking with it. Keep in mind that even heat-treated glass will shatter if you take it from hot to cold too quickly. Since I cool my pies and cakes outside in winter, this is another negative for me.

The Baking Pan List

Two 9"-round cake pans, with 1½"- to 2"-high sides

One 13" x 9" rectangular pan

One 9"-square pan (two are better!)

Two 9" x 5" loaf pans

One 9½"-diameter fluted tart pan with a removable bottom

One standard 12-cup muffin tin

One 13"-diameter Bundt pan (12-cup capacity)

Two to three rimmed baking sheets, approximately 18" x 12"

I don't use silicone pans because they conduct heat differently, which alters browning and bake time. Occasionally, the recipe itself requires changing, which I found with Bundt cakes.

Extras

THERMOMETERS: It's better to be safe than sorry when cooking meat, so you may already have an instant-read or meat thermometer in the house. But thermometers take the guesswork out of making desserts, too. When, say, you're stirring a custard that you know will curdle if it comes to a boil, but you aren't sure the eggs are cooked yet (160°F is done) . . . a thermometer sure comes in handy. Frying, too, is serious business, with low temperatures leading to soggy, oil-laden foods, and a frying thermometer (for high heat) can tell you if you're at the ideal temperature of 365°F or not.

I have only one thermometer in the kitchen, a Polder that has a metal coil attaching the temperature probe to a readout screen. It accommodates high temperatures, and you can program the temperature sensor so that a buzzer will sound when the cooking is done. You can put the probe in and leave the kitchen—the buzzer will let you know when to return. I've worn out one temperature probe and am on my second (with a backup spare ready to go in the drawer). Periodically, check your probe by immersing it in boiling water. If it doesn't register anywhere close to 212°F, it's time to get a new one.

WOODEN SKEWERS: There's no easier way to check for doneness with cakes and muffins than with a wooden pick of some kind. Knives, being smooth, seem to repel batters that are slightly underdone, giving you the impression a cake is done when it is not.

PASTRY BRUSHES: These are handy for brushing melted butter on doughs or for greasing pans. I have several 1" and 2" soft bristle brushes, and one silicone brush to use with hot syrups and glazes.

PYREX OR CERAMIC RAMEKINS: I have a weakness for adorable ramekins. I use them for holding small ingredients that I've measured for a recipe, such as spices, but they are essential for individual desserts like pot de crème, pudding, and mousse.

NUTMEG GRATER: It seems crazy to ask someone to invest in such a specialized tool, but if you bake regularly, you won't regret it. Dried ground nutmeg loses its aroma quickly and has a faintly metallic flavor. I never even liked nutmeg until I grated it fresh, and then I fell in love. And whole nutmegs don't get stale for years—at least mine haven't yet. The savings will pay for the grater.

PLAIN AND STAR PASTRY TIPS: You'll need decorative tips if you like the polished look of piped whipped cream or frosting on desserts. You can use a plain old freezer bag (snip off the corner) to pipe whipped cream or mousse, but you'll need a large pastry bag for stiff doughs like pâte à choux (cream puffs) or spritz cookies.

02

THE UNPLUGGED PANTRY

What You Need to Know About Ingredients

here's an introduction to some of the basic ingredients used in this book. Most entries simply specify a type or brand used in the recipes. There's more science than you'd think behind choosing flour or a type of yeast, so those entries are long. By no means is this list comprehensive—items like buttermilk and sour cream are standard, therefore I didn't feel they warranted further explanation.

BAKING POWDER: All the recipes in this book use double-acting baking powder. *Double-acting* simply means that there are multiple acid components present, usually a fast-acting one that readily reacts with the soda and a slower one that works primarily in the heat of the oven. Baking powders combine acid salts and sodium bicarbonate (baking soda) that react in the presence of liquid and heat, causing the air bubbles present in the batter or dough to expand.

BAKING SODA: Baking soda, or sodium bicarbonate, is one of the few alkaline ingredients in the kitchen. When added to a batter that contains acidic ingredients such as buttermilk, bananas, molasses, or natural cocoa powder, the baking soda will react and release carbon dioxide. Baking soda reacts immediately, so take care not to deflate muffin and cake batters after the soda is initially mixed in and begins its work making bubbles.

BUTTER: All the recipes in this book use unsalted butter. It's not that I'm against salted butter—I actually like the taste of it. But because every brand has a different amount of salt, I find it impossible to get consistent flavor unless I salt my own food. Salt can also mask unsavory flavors that butter develops as it ages or absorbs odors from the refrigerator.

CREAM: Be sure to buy heavy whipping cream for recipes that call for heavy cream. It has nearly 36 percent butterfat, making it possible to whip. At least half the time cream is called for in this book, it will be whipped, so you'll discover very quickly if you bought the wrong kind.

CHOCOLATE: Chopped bittersweet and semisweet chocolate always refer to bars of premium chocolate and not to chocolate chips. Most brands of chocolate chips contain emulsifiers or stabilizers and don't behave the same way as plain bar chocolates. Buy the best chocolate you can.

There is no legal differentiation between bittersweet and semisweet chocolates, so one company's bittersweet could be sweeter than another's semisweet. To compound the confusion, bittersweet bars now come in a variety of seemingly boastful percentages: 55 percent, 65 percent, 75 percent, and even 85 percent cacao or chocolate, the labels read. The recipes in this book use chocolate in the 55 percent to 65 percent range—chocolates with a higher percentage may cause ganache to curdle or mixtures to seize due to their low sugar content.

COCOA POWDER: Cocoa as an ingredient refers to unsweetened cocoa powder, not hot cocoa mixes. There are two types, natural (regular) and Dutch-process (or alkalized). If you don't see a type specified in a recipe, use the one you prefer. Natural cocoas have a robust, almost fruity aroma, like wine. Dutch cocoa has been treated with alkali, which increases its pH, darkens the color from reddish brown to brownish black, and mellows the flavor. If you've ever had an Oreo cookie, you know how velvety and mellow that chocolate flavor is.

Because the pH of each type is different, a specific chemical leavener is paired with each one. For example, cakes that use natural cocoa, which is slightly acidic, may call for a little baking soda, which is alkaline, to neutralize it. Dutch cocoas, already alkalized, are paired with baking powder, which is pH neutral. Just because you use a red cocoa, don't expect a red cake—the finished color depends on the pH of the other cake ingredients, too. Devil's food cake can start with a reddish, natural cocoa but turn almost black thanks to the baking soda.

Though Dutch-process cocoa is often marketed as premium and superior, flavor varies from brand to brand. I prefer Nestlé and Scharffen Berger natural cocoas, and Droste Dutch cocoa. Despite the difference in pH between cocoas, I will occasionally mix the two types together to get the flavor I want.

EGGS: Large eggs are standard in most recipes, including mine. Eggs keep for several weeks in the refrigerator, but be aware that the egg white begins to thin over time. This aspect is most noticeable when making poached eggs, but there's also a pronounced fragility that makes separating egg whites from yolks tricky. See page 26 for more about separating eggs and how to beat egg whites. Occasionally you'll be left with extra egg whites or yolks. These can be frozen for future use. Egg yolks need a bit of salt (⅛ teaspoon for every 4 yolks) beaten into them to prevent them from becoming gummy.

FLOUR: There are two kinds of flour called for in this book, all-purpose and cake flour. All-purpose flour is just what you'd think: a basic flour used for most types of baking. All-purpose flours tend to hover closer to 10 percent to 11 percent protein and are a combination of hard and soft wheat flours, which is good, because we're going to be making mostly cakes and cookies, and the last thing we need is a high protein content to make them strong and tough.

Contrary to popular belief, it makes no difference to your baking whether you choose bleached or unbleached all-purpose flour. Bleached flour will simply make your baked goods whiter. The bleaching agent used for all-purpose flour does not chemically alter the properties of the flour—the strength of the protein will remain unchanged. Cake flour is a different story—its bleaching process *does* change the physical properties of the flour, reducing the strength of the already low protein content. Made from soft, low-protein wheats, cake flour is milled to an ultrafine, almost silky consistency. The pH of cake flour is more acid than that of all-purpose, which means baked goods made with it tend to resist browning. With 8 percent protein or less, cake flour makes light, delicate cakes that all-purpose flour cannot. In fact, some recipes will fail if all-purpose flour is used in its place.

MILK: Unless specified, whole milk is always preferable in baking. The recipes will still work with 2 percent milk, though custards may have a slightly less rich and velvety texture. Do not use 1 percent or skim milk.

MOLASSES: Dark molasses, not blackstrap, is the type most commonly used for baking. If you can find it, buy Barbados-style or any other artisan-style molasses—you'll be pleasantly surprised by the complex smoky and spicy flavors. Muscovado sugar, also called molasses sugar, is a naturally refined, moist dark brown sugar with a high content of this type of molasses. It's so good you can eat it straight.

OIL: When choosing an oil to use for baking, the most important criterion is freshness, as any off or stale flavors and odors will affect the finished flavor of your baked goods. Often the same oil you use for salad dressings and sautéing will be suitable for cakes and cookies, such as corn oil, canola oil, and vegetable oil—just take a whiff of the oil before proceeding with the recipe. Most vegetable oils are comprised of mostly of soy oil. I prefer the clean flavor of safflower oil over soy although it is more expensive. Olive oils, especially the flavor of the lighter varieties, can pair nicely with fruity cakes, like carrot cake, zucchini bread, and even chocolate cakes.

PEANUT BUTTER: I use plain old creamy peanut butter for these recipes—not the natural kind with the oil at the top of the jar. It does have added sugar, and since I have not tested the recipes with both types of peanut butter, I can't predict how the recipes will behave with the natural kind.

SALT: I use plain table salt for all recipes in this book. Table salt is fine grained, making it easy to disperse and dissolve in doughs and batters. Because kosher salt has large, irregularly shaped grains, it doesn't measure as compactly as fine table salt. If you prefer kosher salt, you can use it, but be sure to increase the amount by 25 percent. So, if the recipe calls for 1 teaspoon table salt, you would use 1¼ teaspoons kosher salt. Also, if you use kosher salt, be sure to combine it with the liquids rather than with the dry ingredients, to give it time to dissolve.

SUGAR: I stock granulated sugar, brown sugar, and powdered sugar in my pantry so that I'm ready for any kind of recipe. When a recipe in this book calls for sugar, it means plain old granulated sugar made from sugarcane.

Brown sugar comes in two varieties, light brown and dark brown. If the recipe doesn't specify, use either one. Some recipes recommend specialty sugars, such as the large-grained raw brown sugar (such as demerara) or the very dark and soft muscovado sugar. These sugars are quite expensive, so I've only used them in recipes that show off their unique flavors and textures. Topping rolled and cut cookie dough with demerara sugar adds a delightfully crunchy texture. Save muscovado sugar for icings, custards, and cookies where the brown-sugar flavor is dominant—you won't be able to tell what kind of brown sugar you used in a fudge brownie, for example.

Powdered sugar, also known as confectioners' sugar, is used in some cookie recipes to provide a smooth, fine-grained, nonsandy texture. It is also used to make glazes.

YEAST: All of the recipes in this book were made with fast-acting yeast, which is technically called instant yeast. It is sold in envelopes of three just like regular active dry yeast, but it will specify "fast-acting" on the label. Brand names are Red Star Quick-Rise and Fleischmann's RapidRise. Unlike active dry yeast, instant yeast does not need to be proofed in warm water before it can be used—in fact, proofing it in water isn't good for it. Instead, instant yeast should be mixed directly with the flour. Instant yeast was an improvement on active dry yeast—a different strain of yeast, it also undergoes different processing that makes it hydrate and come to life faster.

If you treat yeast right, it will work fast and never let you down. All yeast works most efficiently in a warm dough (78°F to 80°F is ideal), which is why the water used in bread recipes is warm—usually 115°F or so. Temperatures above 140°F will kill the yeast, and cool temperatures will prevent it from hydrating properly and also flat out kill the yeast. Once the yeast is hydrated, however, it's fine to cool the dough down.

Yeast, like some of my relatives, doesn't like to be near a lot of sugar, salt, or fat—all these ingredients will slow it down. You'll notice that high-sugar and high-fat bread doughs use a lot of yeast to compensate—a simple baguette made from flour, water, yeast, and salt uses less yeast. Most of my sweet dough recipes have a 15-minute sponge of all the water or milk, about half the flour, and the yeast. The butter, sugar, eggs, and salt are added in a second mixing stage. This lets the yeast get a jump start and keeps the rising times relatively short.

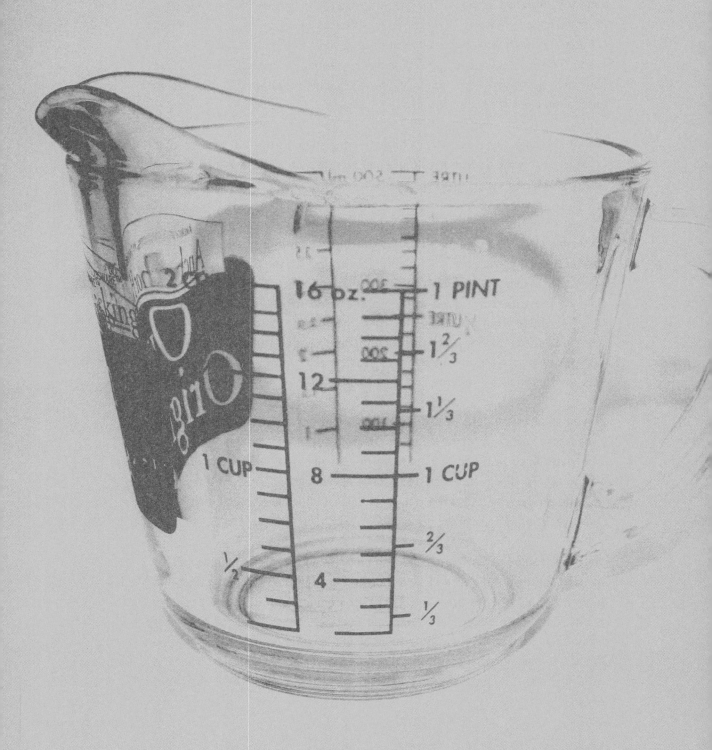

03.

THE
BASICS

How to Read a Recipe

for those who don't venture into the kitchen to bake often, this section is a refresher course on how to navigate a recipe, particularly the ones in this book. An ingredient list, for example, is more than just a list of measurements. When you look more closely, you'll find the wording implies that certain actions have already been completed—½ cup toasted pecans, chopped, means that the nuts have been measured, chopped, and toasted. Three steps in one short line! It's always a good idea to read ahead before embarking on a new recipe. The mistakes I make in baking are almost always because I stopped reading and skipped ahead.

Ingredients are listed in the order they will be used.

If an ingredient will be used more than once, you'll see the word *divided* after it. Read the text carefully to make sure you put the right amount in.

If brown sugar is listed as an ingredient, either dark or light is fine. Otherwise the recipe will say so.

Many recipes call for toasted nuts. To toast nuts, spread them on a rimmed baking sheet and bake them at 350°F until golden and fragrant. For room-temperature nuts, this could be anywhere from 5 minutes for walnuts to 8 or 10 minutes for almonds. Naturally, frozen nuts take longer to bake. Hazelnuts usually come with papery skins that will rub off after baking.

There is a difference between "1 cup finely chopped pecans" and "1 cup pecans, finely chopped." The comma means to measure out the pecans first, then chop them.

Soft butter has been sitting at room temperature long enough to be pliable. To quicken the process, dice the amount of butter called for and leave it on a plate—small pieces warm up faster. You can even place the plate near a warm oven. Like my grandmother, I leave my butter on the counter 24 hours a day during the cooler months, so I'm always ready to bake.

If a recipe calls for room-temperature eggs, you can immerse whole, cold eggs in a bowl of warm water and they'll be ready in a minute or two. With cakes and muffins, you'll get better volume and emulsification (Don't you hate batters that looks curdled?) with a warm (70°F to 80°F) batter. I typically use cold eggs in cookie doughs because the primary function of the eggs is not to add volume to the cookies and because cold doughs spread less. If you have to chill the dough later, why not keep it as cool as possible during the mixing?

Unless you need to chill a cookie dough or wait for dough to rise, it's always best to start every recipe by preheating the oven so that it's ready when you are.

After preheating the oven, preparing your baking pan is the next thing to do before proceeding with making the recipe. If a recipe says to butter and flour a pan, use whatever fat was called for in the recipe—so if it's an oil-based cake, brush the pan with oil. The exception to this would be nonstick bakeware, whose slick surface causes oil or melted butter to bead up. Brushed solid shortening or soft butter adheres better to those pans.

Measuring Basics

Use the dry measuring cups for dry ingredients and the liquid cups for wet ones. If you can't figure out which category you're dealing with (peanut butter, for example), use either one.

Measure flour by spooning it into the measuring cup and using an offset spatula to sweep off the excess. This "spoon and sweep" method is standard in baking.

Scoop granulated sugar into the measuring cup—spooning it gently makes no difference—and pack brown sugar tightly into measuring cups. Because it compacts easily, you should measure powdered sugar just like flour for accuracy.

When measuring liquids, be sure to place the glass on a level surface and bend to look at the glass at eye level for accuracy.

When measuring leaveners or other small-quantity items with measuring spoons, simply scoop the spoon through the ingredient and level it off with the flat edge of a knife or an offset spatula.

Basic Techniques

A few techniques are so commonplace in baking that they are seldom singled out for explanation within the recipe. Rather than include the details of how to whip cream or explain why the leavener is usually added to the flour each time, I've provided the details below, along with the logic behind the techniques.

MELTING CHOCOLATE: Very few recipes in this book call for melting chocolate alone. I try to avoid it, because it's so much easier to melt chocolate with something else, like butter or cream. Why? Because chocolate burns easily at temperatures well under the boiling point (160°F is too hot for it). To safely melt chocolate, make a double boiler: Fill a small pan with about an inch of water and bring it to a boil. Reduce the temperature so that the water is at a gentle simmer. Place a metal bowl over the pan so that it rests on top. Choose a bowl that is just a bit wider than the pan, so that it nestles nicely. Place the chopped chocolate in the bowl, and stir occasionally with a rubber spatula until melted and smooth. Take care not to let the water boil too vigorously or to let steam condense inside the bowl with the chocolate. Although chocolate can be melted with large amounts of liquid, a few drops of water will cause it to seize. There is no fix for chocolate that has seized, except to add cream and simply turn it into ganache.

SEPARATING EGGS: Many recipes call for separating the yolk from the egg white. It is impossible to properly whip an egg white that has come into contact with fat, so you'll need to take care not to let the yolk break during this process. Start with cold eggs for greatest ease—once the eggs become warm, the yolks break easily.

First, break the egg into a small bowl, holding it near the bottom of the bowl so that the egg slides gently out of the shell into the bowl. Next, gently scoop the yolk into your fingers, letting the white fall away. Place the yolk into another small bowl, then pour the egg white into a larger bowl, the one in which you'll whip the whites. Repeat as necessary. It may seem redundant to transfer the egg white to a different bowl, but if you were to leave the whites in the bowl into which you continue to break eggs, you risk having a yolk break and contaminate many egg whites, not just one.

After you've separated the eggs, you can let them sit and come to room temperature. This is important for egg whites, which form the greatest volume of foam when warm. To speed this process along, you can place the bowl of egg whites in a sink filled with hot water and whisk them for a minute or until no longer cold.

WHIPPING EGG WHITES: Egg whites are surprisingly fast and easy to whip. Be sure to start with warm whites for the greatest volume. Adding a few drops of lemon juice or a half a teaspoon of cream of tartar—both acids— will help stabilize the egg foam, but they are not absolutely necessary. I like to beat the eggs until they are at the soft-peak stage (the foam will hold soft peaks that curl over at the tips when the whisk is pulled away from the whites) and then slowly beat in sugar until the whites almost hold stiff peaks (the tips can almost stand up straight when the whisk is pulled away). This makes a stable egg foam that can withstand being folded into a batter without deflating. Once you've added sugar, the foam is technically called a meringue, but I just call it foolproof egg whites. Most recipes ask for you to stir or fold in a small amount of the whipped egg whites to "lighten" the batter before adding the remaining whipped egg whites. This step helps minimize how much the egg foam is deflated during the folding process.

WHIPPING CREAM: Whipping cream is by far the hardest thing you'll do in this entire book, unless you decide to cheat and use an electric mixer. You can also use old-fashioned hand-cranked egg beaters, but it's still a job. Pre-chilling the bowl and whisk is helpful, but whipping in a cool environment is even better—cold air encourages the fat globules in cream to hold together as a foam. I whisk cream outside in winter for this reason. In summer, if I have to whip more than a cup of cream, I'll admit it, I reach for a hand mixer. If you intend to whip cream by hand, do yourself a favor and avoid ultrapasteurized heavy whipping cream. Sure, it keeps longer in the refrigerator before going bad, but it's a lot harder to whip—a point unmistakable when you are beating by hand. You can shave 3 to 4 minutes off the beating time by using regular heavy whipping cream.

On the next two pages are some general guidelines for mixing and baking. Detailed explanations for mixing batters and folding ingredients together can be found at the beginning of Chapters 6 and 8, respectively.

Mixing Basics

Most recipes say to combine the dry ingredients together first. This ensures that small-quantity items such as salt and baking powder will get evenly dispersed in the batter or dough. Occasionally, I'll add the salt to the egg mixture if I know that there will be very little stirring once the flour is added.

Because leaveners are sensitive to moisture and will begin to react in a batter, I like to thoroughly mix them with the flour before adding them to batters. Cookie doughs are different, since they can handle a lot more stirring without creating toughness, so often I get lazy and merely dump the salt and baking soda on top of the flour and then stir.

When making cakes, usually the flour and liquids are added alternately in quick, efficient additions meant to prevent the cake from becoming tough. You start with the flour, because coating it with the fat inhibits the formation of gluten, a protein that creates toughness in cakes. Don't wait for one thing to be perfectly mixed in before dumping in the next item—that would take a lot more stirring than is desirable.

Baking Basics

Unless a recipe specifies otherwise, place pans on a rack in the center of the oven.

When baking cookies, or anything that won't fit on one centrally placed oven rack, you'll need to arrange two racks evenly in the oven. You'll get more consistent baking if the racks are located toward the center of the oven rather placed near the top and bottom. Just be sure to leave adequate space between the racks for good air circulation.

If you are baking on two racks, be sure to switch the pans top to bottom halfway through the baking.

The heat source is almost always at the bottom of the oven. Foods like soufflés, cream puffs, and puff pastry do well starting out near the bottom of the oven—the initial burst of heat they'll get as soon as you close the oven door helps them to rise.

Because scones, shortcakes, and biscuits tend to brown faster on the bottom sides than on the tops, it's a good idea to bake them in the top third of the oven, where the heat rises and hovers. Baking them on two sheet pans stacked together (double-panning) also inhibits bottom browning.

04

TREATS FOR THE FIRST HALF OF THE DAY

baking isn't just about dessert, as this recipe-packed chapter demonstrates. Breakfast, brunch, and coffee-break treats can significantly improve one's quality of living. I know homemade granola has made my workday mornings better, just like rustic fruit galettes make leisurely weekend mornings that much more luxurious. Here's where you'll find traditional favorites like Southern-Style Pull-Apart Biscuits and Sticky Buns, as well as some wonderful, easy dishes that most of us don't make often enough, like Clafouti, Popovers, and Plum and Blackberry Kuchen.

breakfast
favorites

Uncommonly Good Pancakes

These are my company pancakes—delicate, light, and never leaden (for every-day pancakes that are a bit less rich, see the following recipe). The secret to the fine texture is both the cake flour and the emulsifying action of the extra egg yolks. For a rich, complex flavor, I add a few drops of almond extract to the batter—this tiny amount enhances the buttery flavor without imparting a discernable almond flavor. If you like thinner pancakes, add more milk. For thicker ones, add a tablespoon or two more flour. Be sure to have the milk and eggs at room temperature or the butter will harden. If you use oil instead of butter, however, cold ingredients are fine.

MAKES SIXTEEN 4" PANCAKES.

1½ C. all-purpose flour	3 Tbs. sugar
¾ C. cake flour	2 large egg yolks
2 tsp. baking powder	2 large eggs, at room temperature
½ tsp. salt	2 C. buttermilk, at room temperature
¼ tsp. baking soda	½ tsp. vanilla extract
6 Tbs. unsalted butter, melted	⅛ tsp. almond extract (optional)

In a small bowl, whisk together the flours, baking powder, salt, and baking soda. In another bowl, whisk the melted butter with the sugar and egg yolks until smooth. Whisk in the two whole eggs, beating vigorously for 30 seconds. Whisk in the buttermilk and the extracts. Pour the flour mixture over the egg mixture and gently stir just until combined. Let the batter stand for 5 to 10 minutes before using—this lets the gluten relax and the flour hydrate, and makes for perfectly tender pancakes.

Cook for 3 to 5 minutes (depending on whether you make silver dollar–sized cakes or larger ones) on a hot, greased griddle or skillet set over medium heat, turning once. The pancakes are ready to turn when the sides begin to set and bubbles form across the top surface. Keep the pancakes covered and warm until ready to serve, or, even better, serve as they come off the griddle.

Both buttery and nutty, wheat germ waffles were a Saturday morning ritual when I was a kid. Yes, even wheat germ didn't deter us kids from consuming piles of them. The batter is a cinch to put together and will keep overnight if you have extra, though that's unlikely. You can freeze cooked waffles and crisp them in a hot oven later, sort of like frozen toaster waffles. This recipe makes great pancakes, too. Adding more milk will make a thinner pancake. Be sure to have the milk and eggs at room temperature or the butter will seize and harden into lumps. Yes, there is such thing as a stove-top waffle iron, so waffles, too, can be unplugged.

MAKES ABOUT 12 STANDARD WAFFLES (OR ABOUT 16 4" PANCAKES).

2 C. all-purpose flour

¼ C. toasted wheat germ

2 tsp. baking powder

½ tsp. baking soda

½ tsp. salt

3 large eggs, at room temperature

6 Tbs. unsalted butter, melted,
  or ⅓ C. oil

3 Tbs. sugar

2 C. buttermilk, at room temperature

½ tsp. vanilla extract

⅛ tsp. almond extract (optional)

In a small bowl, whisk together the flour, wheat germ, baking powder, baking soda, and salt. In another bowl, vigorously whisk the melted butter with the eggs and sugar until smooth and slightly fluffy, about 30 seconds. Stir in the buttermilk and the extracts. Pour the flour mixture over the eggs and gently stir just until combined. Let the batter stand for 5 to 10 minutes before using—this lets the gluten relax, preventing tough waffles.

Cook the waffles in a greased, preheated waffle iron according to manufacturer's instructions. If you no longer have the instructions, follow the old adage that waffles are done when the flow of steam from the waffle iron slows. This is usually 1½ to 3 minutes, depending on how crisp you like your waffles. Waffles quickly lose their crispy edges, so hold in a 300°F to 350°F oven (right on the rack) if not serving immediately.

→ **HAZELNUT WAFFLES:** Omit the wheat germ and add ¼ cup toasted, skinned hazelnuts that have been finely ground using a rotary cheese grater.

Clafouti

Clafouti is a weekend ritual in my house, usually thrown together while brewing a second pot of coffee and getting ready to settle into the Sunday paper. If you have 20 minutes (including baking time!), you could make this every day for breakfast. It may sound fancy and foreign, but clafouti is simply a sweetened egg custard packed with fruit. In France they are eaten for dessert, but a John Thorne essay got me hooked on them for breakfast. Though his recipe is just about perfect, I have a bit more of a sweet tooth, so I've added a bit more sugar, vanilla, and brandy to mine. Tart fruit works best—depending on the season I use raspberries, chopped plums, pitted cherries, or cranberries. In winter I often use dried tart cherries or prunes that I have steeped in brandy or amaretto. If you like textural contrast, try sprinkling 2 tablespoons toasted sliced almonds and 1 tablespoon sugar over the batter before it goes into the oven.

MAKES 3 TO 4 SERVINGS.

½ C. all-purpose flour

¼ C. sugar, divided (for cranberries, double the sugar)

¼ tsp. salt

3 large eggs

1 C. (scant) whole or 2% milk

½ tsp. vanilla extract

⅛ tsp. almond extract (optional)

1 Tbs. unsalted butter

1½ C. fresh fruit, such as pitted cherries or raspberries

3 Tbs. brandy, amaretto, Grand Marnier, or Cointreau—whatever you have on hand

Powdered sugar, for dusting

Preheat the oven to 425°F. Place an ovenproof 9" or 10" skillet over medium heat for a minute or two to get hot. Meanwhile, in a medium bowl, whisk together the flour, 2 tablespoons of the sugar, and the salt. Gradually whisk in the eggs until the mixture is smooth and lump free. Whisk in the milk and extracts.

Melt the butter in the hot skillet, swirling to coat evenly. Sprinkle the remaining sugar over the butter and then add the fruit to the pan. Increase the heat to medium-high and sauté, shaking the pan frequently, until the fruit softens and the juices and sugar form a thick syrup, about 3 minutes for most fruit, longer for cranberries.

Turn off the heat and add the brandy to the pan, shaking the pan to coat the fruit evenly. Pour the egg batter into the pan. Bake in the upper third of the oven for 10 to 12 minutes, until puffed on the sides and fully cooked in the center (check with the tip of a knife). Serve warm with a dusting of powdered sugar.

Popovers

Once upon a time I thought I needed a fancy popover pan to make these crispy puffs, but I lost the pan long ago and have been using my standard 12-cup muffin pan ever since. Popovers are one of my favorite weekend morning treats, just as satisfying as pastry, but quicker and lighter. In summer I serve them with fresh berries and whipped cream, and in cooler months a heartier warm fruit compote with crème fraîche or mascarpone whipped cream. I've also added grated cheese, herbs, and black pepper to the batter and served them with dinner. Try dry mustard and dill, or cheddar and black pepper popovers—they will surprise and delight your family and friends and they are shockingly easy to prepare.

MAKES ABOUT 12 POPOVERS.

1 C. all-purpose flour

2 tsp. sugar

¼ tsp. plus ⅛ tsp. salt

2 large eggs

2 Tbs. unsalted butter, melted

1 C. plus 2 Tbs. milk

Preheat the oven to 450°F. Brush the bottom, sides, and top of a 12-cup muffin tin with melted butter. In a small bowl, whisk together the flour, sugar, and salt. Beat in the eggs and melted butter until the mixture is smooth and lump free, adding some of the milk to make the stirring easier if necessary. Whisk in the remaining milk. Divide the batter evenly among the muffin cups. If you happen to end up one muffin cup short, fill it halfway with water so the pan does not burn. Bake for 15 minutes, then, without opening the oven, reduce the oven temperature to 350°F. Bake for another 20 minutes or so or until the tops are golden and crisp. Run a knife around the edges of the popovers to loosen and transfer them to a wire rack to cool. Puncture the bottoms with a sharp knife to let steam escape—this will help them stay crisp. Serve immediately.

Dutch Baby

Also called a German pancake, a Dutch baby is sort of a cross between a popover and a clafouti, with a texture similar to Yorkshire pudding. The "Dutch" moniker refers to the German settlers we call Pennsylvania Dutch, and the "baby"—well, your guess is as good as mine. Rising and puffing impressively as it bakes, the baby begins to fall as it's removed from the oven. Drizzled with lemon juice, melted butter, and a healthy dusting of powdered sugar, a Dutch baby is served hot, right in its ovenproof skillet. Traditionally it's accompanied by sautéed, lightly sweetened fruit, such as apples, but a side of sour cream or whipped cream isn't unheard of. For those who don't cook or bake often, this old-fashioned recipe is simple and rewarding enough to make it a weekend tradition.

MAKES 3 TO 4 SERVINGS.

¾ C. all-purpose flour	2 large eggs
2 Tbs. sugar	3 Tbs. unsalted butter, divided
¼ tsp. salt	2 Tbs. fresh lemon juice
¾ C. milk (not skim)	Powdered sugar for dusting

Preheat the oven to 425°F. In a medium bowl, whisk together the flour, sugar, and salt. In another medium bowl, whisk together the milk, eggs, and 1 tablespoon of the butter (melted) until well combined. Gradually whisk two-thirds of the wet ingredients into the dry ingredients to eliminate any lumps, and then whisk in the remaining liquid until the mixture is smooth.

Place an ovenproof 9" to 10" skillet over medium heat for a minute or two to get hot. Melt the remaining 2 tablespoons butter in the hot skillet, swirling to coat evenly. Pour the egg batter into the pan. Bake in the upper third of the oven for 18 to 20 minutes, until puffed and very well browned at the edges and golden on top. An underbaked Dutch baby will be unappealingly soggy and moist. Serve warm, drizzled with the lemon juice and with a dusting of powdered sugar.

Chocolate Chip Muffins

Moist and rich with sour cream, these muffins are great with your morning coffee or a cold glass of milk. Don't be fooled by the presence of chocolate—these muffins aren't nearly as sweet and light as a dessert cake. But for those of you who love to start your morning with a bit of chocolate, they are a great alternative to all the typical fruit-laden morning foods.

MAKES 1 DOZEN MEDIUM MUFFINS OR 10 LARGE MUFFINS.

1⅓ C. all-purpose flour

⅔ C. cake flour

¾ tsp. baking powder

¾ tsp. baking soda

¼ tsp. plus ⅛ tsp. salt

¼ C. unsalted butter, soft

⅔ C. sugar

2 large eggs, at room temperature

1 tsp. vanilla extract

1 C. sour cream, at room temperature

¾ C. mini chocolate chips or finely
    chopped semisweet bar chocolate

Preheat the oven to 375°F. Butter and flour a standard 12-cup muffin pan for medium muffins or a 10-cup muffin pan for larger ones. In a medium bowl whisk together the flours, baking powder, baking soda, and salt until well combined. In another bowl beat the butter and sugar until smooth, 1 to 2 minutes. One at a time, whisk in the eggs, then the vanilla; the batter will look a little curdled. Stir in half the flour mixture and then the sour cream. Dump the remaining flour mixture into the bowl, place the mini chocolate chips on top, and then gently stir until the batter just barely comes together. (A rubber spatula works great for this because you can fold the batter up and over easily without overmixing the batter.) Divide the batter evenly among the muffin cups. Bake for 16 to 20 minutes or until a wooden skewer inserted in the top of a muffin comes out clean. Let cool in the pan for 2 to 3 minutes. Transfer the muffins to a wire rack to cool as soon as you can comfortably remove them from the pan.

Blueberry Muffins

In most coffee shops and bakeries, muffins are merely small, rich cakes—too sweet, fattening, and dense to accompany my cup of morning coffee. For tender, light, and not-too-sweet muffins, you have to make your own. This recipe has the open crumb I associate with a good muffin. If you like tart lemon flavor, brush the tops of the muffins with the optional syrup—it's a much better bet than adding lemon juice to the batter, which will turn the blueberry juices green. Frozen berries may be used, but you will need to thaw them under running warm water (not hot) until the water runs clear and drain them well on paper towels. Since frozen berries collapse as they thaw, measure out a little more than the recipe calls for.

MAKES 1 DOZEN MUFFINS.

2¾ C. all-purpose flour
1 Tbs. baking powder
½ tsp. baking soda
½ tsp. salt
¾ C. unsalted butter, soft
1 C. sugar
Grated zest of 1 large lemon

2 large eggs, at room temperature
¼ C. water
½ tsp. vanilla extract (optional)
1 C. plain yogurt (anything but nonfat)
1½ to 2 C. blueberries

Preheat the oven to 375°F. Butter and flour a standard 12-cup muffin pan. In a medium bowl, whisk together the flour, baking powder, baking soda, and salt. In another bowl, beat the butter, sugar, and lemon zest until smooth, 1 to 2 minutes. One at a time, whisk in the eggs. Whisk in the water and vanilla; the batter will look a little curdled. Stir in half the flour mixture, then the yogurt. Dump the remaining flour mixture into the bowl, place the berries on top, and then gently stir until the batter just barely comes together. (A silicone spatula works great for this because you can fold the batter up and over easily without breaking the berries or overmixing the batter.) Divide the batter evenly among the muffin cups—they will be nearly full—don't worry. Bake for 18 to 22 minutes or until a wooden skewer inserted in the top of a muffin comes out clean. Let cool in the pan for 2 to 3 minutes. Transfer the muffins to a wire rack to cool as soon as you can comfortably remove them from the pan. If desired, brush lemon syrup over the still-warm muffins.

→ **OPTIONAL LEMON SYRUP:** Bring ¼ cup lemon juice and 3 tablespoons sugar to a boil over medium-high heat. Boil for 1 to 2 minutes or until the sugar has dissolved and the mixture is syrupy.

→ **RASPBERRY OR BLACKBERRY MUFFINS:** Omit the lemon zest and add ⅛ teaspoon almond extract. Substitute 1½ cups fresh raspberries or blackberries for the blueberries. Since these muffins are tarter than the blueberry ones, I like to top them with a white streusel: In a small bowl, combine ⅔ cup all-purpose flour, ½ cup sugar, ⅓ cup finely chopped toasted almonds (optional), ¼ teaspoon ground allspice, and ⅛ teaspoon salt. With your fingers, work in ¼ cup soft butter until the mixture clumps when pressed between your fingers. Sprinkle the streusel over the batter before baking.

Cranberry-Orange Muffins

I adore cranberries. Without them, I'd go berry-less through the winter months. Their tartness puts off some folks, but that refreshing zing makes them perfect for baking. Desserts made with them are never cloyingly sweet. In this muffin, the classic cranberry-orange flavor combination gets an added boost from ground ginger. If you like ginger, consider adding finely minced crystallized ginger for really intense flavor. This recipe can also be easily adapted to make a loaf quick bread, very nice sliced and fanned on a plate for a morning coffee break. Note that although many muffin recipes can be made into quick breads by merely baking them in a loaf pan, you must decrease the liquid in this recipe to produce a loaf firm enough to slice (see the recipe variation, below).

MAKES 1 DOZEN MEDIUM MUFFINS.

2 C. all-purpose flour
½ C. cake flour
2 tsp. baking powder
1 tsp. ground ginger
½ tsp. baking soda
½ tsp. salt
10 Tbs. unsalted butter, soft
¾ C. plus 2 Tbs. sugar

2 large eggs, at room temperature
1½ tsp. grated orange zest
1 tsp. vanilla extract
1 C. buttermilk, at room temperature
¼ C. fresh orange juice
1½ C. fresh (or slightly thawed frozen) cranberries, coarsely chopped

NOTE: Instead of the orange juice and zest, you may use 1 teaspoon pure orange oil. Increase the buttermilk by ¼ cup to make up the difference in liquid.

Preheat the oven to 425°F. Butter and flour a 12-cup muffin pan. In a medium bowl, whisk together the flours, baking powder, ginger, baking soda, and salt until well combined. In another bowl, beat the butter and sugar until smooth, 1 to 2 minutes. One at a time, whisk in the eggs, then the orange zest and vanilla. Stir in half the flour mixture and then the buttermilk and orange juice. Dump the remaining flour mixture into the bowl, place the chopped cranberries on top, and then gently stir until the batter just barely comes together. (A silicone spatula works great for this because you can fold the batter up and over easily without breaking the berries or overmixing the batter.)

Divide the batter evenly among the muffin cups. Bake for 15 to 17 minutes or until a wooden skewer inserted in the top of a muffin comes out clean. Let cool in the pan for 2 to 3 minutes. Transfer the muffins to a wire rack to cool as soon as you can comfortably remove them from the pan.

→ **CRANBERRY-ORANGE BREAD:** Reduce the amount of buttermilk by ¼ cup. Bake the batter in a buttered and floured 9" x 5" loaf pan at 350°F for 55 to 60 minutes or until a wooden skewer inserted in the center of the loaf comes out clean.

Bran Cereal Muffins

Why bother with bran cereal when you can have a tasty bran muffin instead? Soaking the cereal in the buttermilk makes for a tender, light, and moist muffin—not at all dense or chewy like most bran muffins. I love serving them with honey-butter and a side of bacon—a perfect combination of sweet, salty, and savory flavors. They are terribly addictive and I am always a little worried when I watch company toss back three or four of them. After all, most of us wouldn't eat three or four bowls of bran cereal. Like most muffins, these are best the day they are made, but they hold up well in the freezer if you have any leftovers.

MAKES 12 SMALL MUFFINS OR 10 TO 11 GOOD-SIZED ONES.

1¾ C. buttermilk

⅓ C. oil

1 large egg

⅓ C. packed brown sugar

2 C. All-Bran cereal

1¼ C. all-purpose flour

1½ tsp. baking powder

1 tsp. baking soda

¼ tsp. plus ⅛ tsp. salt

½ C. raisins (optional)

Preheat the oven to 425°F. Butter and flour a 12-cup muffin pan. In a medium bowl, whisk together the buttermilk, oil, egg, and sugar until smooth. Stir in the cereal and soak for about 15 minutes—the cereal will swell and soften in the liquid. In another medium bowl, whisk together the flour, baking powder, baking soda, and salt until well combined. Stir in the raisins if desired. Gently fold the flour mixture into the cereal mixture until just combined. The batter will thicken almost immediately as the baking soda reacts with the buttermilk. Do not stir after this point to avoid deflating the batter. Gently scoop the batter into the muffin cups. Bake for 12 to 14 minutes or until a wooden skewer inserted into the center of one comes out clean. Let cool in the pan for 2 to 3 minutes. Transfer the muffins to a wire rack to cool as soon as you can comfortably remove them from the pan.

Maple Oat Muffins

Oats and dark maple syrup combine to make a tasty breakfast muffin that's sensibly healthy and not too fattening. The secret to their moist texture is soaking the oats in the buttermilk for at least 15 minutes before making the muffins. Be sure to use regular rolled oats (usually labeled "old-fashioned") and not the quick rolled oats—the quick oats will disintegrate into mush. I use Grade B dark amber maple syrup because it has a deeper flavor that's less likely to be overpowered by other ingredients.

MAKES 12 SMALL MUFFINS.

1¼ C. buttermilk
⅓ C. Grade B maple syrup
⅓ C. oil
⅓ C. packed light brown sugar
2 large eggs
1⅔ C. old-fashioned rolled oats
½ C. dried fruit (golden raisins or

diced dried apple slices are
excellent)
1¼ C. all-purpose flour
2 tsp. baking powder
1 tsp. baking soda
¾ tsp. salt
¼ tsp. ground cinnamon

Preheat the oven to 425°F. Butter and flour a 12-cup muffin pan. In a medium bowl, whisk together the buttermilk, maple syrup, oil, brown sugar, and eggs until smooth. Stir in the oats and soak for about 15 minutes—the oats will soften in the liquid. Stir in the dried fruit. In another medium bowl, whisk together the flour, baking powder, baking soda, salt, and cinnamon until well combined. Gently fold the flour mixture into the oat mixture until just combined. The batter will thicken almost immediately as the baking soda reacts with the buttermilk. Do not stir after this point to avoid deflating the batter. Gently scoop the batter into the muffin cups. The cups will be very full—don't worry. Bake for 13 to 15 minutes or until a wooden skewer inserted into the center of one comes out clean. Let cool in the pan for 2 to 3 minutes. Transfer the muffins to a wire rack to cool as soon as you can comfortably remove them from the pan.

Summer Fruit Breakfast Galette, Two Ways

Yes, a galette is sort of a rustic pie, and yes, at my house it's considered break-fast. I think this galette is one of the better ways to enjoy summer's bounty—a crisp-tender, flaky golden crust packed with ripe, juicy fruit.

If you have a pizza stone, feel free to use it in place of the preheated baking sheet, but honestly, either one works just fine. Rolling out galette dough on parchment paper is a handy trick that makes it feasible to transfer a filled galette to the preheated baking sheet (key in achieving that crispy bottom crust). If you don't have parchment, just roll the dough out on a floured sur-face and transfer it to a floured cutting board before adding the fruit and fold-ing the edges. You should be able to use the cutting board like a baker's peel and just slide the galette right onto the hot pan in the oven. A preheated bak-ing surface causes the tart edges to firm up quickly so that you won't lose any delicious fruit to spillage.

Two variations for crust are given here. I usually use the cornmeal version with berries (any combination of blueberries, blackberries, raspberries, or cherries) and the walnut version with stone fruit (such as apricots, plums, peaches, or nectarines). The cornmeal dough was inspired by Flo Braker's wonderful galette, the recipe for which was published in *Baking with Julia* by Dorie Greenspan.

Each dough recipe makes enough for two crusts: You can have a galette two days in a row if you refrigerate the spare disk, or freeze it for the next time you go berry or peach picking. It's not a good idea to use all the dough for one large galette—the fruit mixture will not thicken by the time the edges of the pastry are brown and crisp.

NOTES: You can use frozen fruit, but the baking time will be longer, and you won't need to preheat the baking sheet. The amount of sugar called for here is what you'll need with ripe fruit. If the fruit is a bit underripe or on the tart side, increase the sugar by a few tablespoons.

EACH GALETTE SERVES 4.

CORNMEAL OR WALNUT GALETTE DOUGH

1 C. plus 2 Tbs. all-purpose flour

¼ C. fine yellow cornmeal (or ¼ cup walnut halves)

1 Tbs. sugar

½ tsp. salt

½ C. cold unsalted butter

¼ C. sour cream

¼ C. ice-cold water

BERRY FILLING

⅓ C. sugar

2 Tbs. cornstarch

¼ tsp. ground cinnamon

⅛ tsp. ground allspice

Pinch of salt

2½ to 3 C. mixed berries (blueberries, raspberries, blackberries, or cherries)

STONE FRUIT FILLING

⅓ C. sugar

1½ Tbs. cornstarch

¼ tsp. ground ginger

Grating of fresh nutmeg

Pinch of salt

2½ to 3 C. sliced stone fruit (nectarines, peaches, plums, apricots, or any combination

Sugar for sprinkling

Preheat the oven to 425°F with a large baking sheet or pizza stone on the center rack. For the cornmeal dough, in a large bowl, whisk together the flour, cornmeal, sugar, and salt until well combined. Using the medium shredding holes on a box grater, grate the butter into the flour, tossing often to coat the butter with flour. Using a pastry blender or your fingers, work the butter into the flour until it forms ¼" pieces. Stir together the sour cream and ice water. With a fork, gently stir enough of the liquid into the dry mixture until the dough just begins to clump together. You will still want to have a few stray crumbly bits that are not fully incorporated. Don't overmix or the dough will not be flaky. Divide the dough in half and form into two disks. Wrap in plastic and chill for 15 minutes or so while you make the filling. (This rest time makes the dough easy to roll without overworking or stretching.) For walnut dough, chop the walnuts very finely or grind them in a rotary cheese grater. Reduce the amount of butter by 1 tablespoon and proceed as above.

For either fruit filling, in a medium bowl, whisk together the dry ingredients. Add the fruit and toss to coat evenly; set aside. On a sheet of parchment paper or well-floured surface, roll out one disk of either dough into a 12" circle, dusting with flour as needed to prevent sticking. Don't worry if the edges are rough or uneven—this is a rustic tart! Brush off any excess flour from both sides of the dough circle with a pastry brush. Spoon the fruit into the center of the circle, leaving a 3" border. Fold the edges of the dough over the fruit to cover, pleating as you go around and pressing lightly to set. There will be a gap in the middle of 2" to 4" that is not covered by dough. Lightly brush the top of galette with water using a pastry brush and sprinkle heavily with sugar. Transfer the parchment with the tart to the baking sheet or stone (or use the above-mentioned trick with a cutting board). Bake for 35 to 40 minutes or until the fruit is bubbling in the center and the pastry is golden. Slide immediately off the baking pan onto a wire rack to cool, removing the parchment in order to keep the crust crisp. Let cool for at least 15 minutes, but serve while warm. A side of ice cream turns this into a lovely dessert.

Southern-Style Pull-Apart Biscuits

Lots of recipes promise moist, tender biscuits but just don't deliver the fluffy, pull-apart biscuits I remember from my childhood in the Midwest. This recipe equals my memories and does them one better. Half cake flour makes for a tender and fluffy biscuit, while the high amount of buttermilk makes them moist.

MAKES 15 BISCUITS.

1½ C. cake flour	½ tsp. baking soda
2 C. all-purpose flour (divided)	¾ C. cold unsalted butter
2 Tbs. sugar	1½ C. cold buttermilk
1 Tbs. baking powder	1 to 2 Tbs. unsalted butter, melted,
1 tsp. salt	for brushing the biscuits

Preheat the oven to 375°F. Butter a 13" x 9" baking pan. In a large bowl, stir together the cake flour, 1½ cups of the all-purpose flour, the sugar, baking powder, salt, and baking soda until well combined. Using the medium shredding holes on a box grater, grate the butter into the flour, tossing often to coat the butter with flour. Using a pastry blender or your fingers, work the butter into the flour until it forms ¼" pieces. Gently fold in the buttermilk until the flour is mostly incorporated. Don't overmix—the batter will be thick, sticky, and lumpy.

Place the remaining ½ cup flour in a small bowl. Scoop about ⅓ cup of dough into the dusting flour, rolling the dough to coat it evenly. Gently roll or pat the dough into a round ball and drop into the pan. Repeat this procedure with the remaining dough, 5 biscuits the long way in the pan and 3 the short way, leaving small gaps between the dough balls. Press the tops to flatten slightly and brush them with the melted butter. Bake in the upper third of the oven for 18 to 22 minutes or until no longer doughy in the center and browned on the tops.

→ **CINNAMON BISCUITS:** Omit the dusting flour and use a combination of ¼ cup packed light brown sugar, 2 tablespoons all-purpose flour, 1 teaspoon ground cinnamon, and ⅛ teaspoon salt to coat the dough pieces. After brushing the tops with butter, top with the remaining cinnamon-sugar.

Honey Granola

Granola over yogurt is my weekday breakfast during the summer. Because I am particular about what flavors I like, I find it's best to make it myself. With all the stuff you could add to granola, the variations are endless, so make this recipe your own. The basic formula is just barely sweet and light on the oil—many other granola recipes are surprisingly high in fat. The trick to great granola is baking the mixture slowly, so that it dries out before it gets too brown. Check the mixture frequently, and if it seems to be browning too much, reduce the oven temperature by 50°F.

MAKES ABOUT 7 CUPS GRANOLA.

½ C. sugar
1 large egg white
3 Tbs. oil
2 Tbs. honey
2 Tbs. water
1 tsp. vanilla extract
½ tsp. salt
4 C. old-fashioned rolled oats

1½ C. dried fruit, such as raisins, cherries, blueberries, cranberries, coconut, or chopped apricots, dates, figs, or pineapple
1½ C. mixed toasted nuts and seeds, such as walnuts, almonds, hazelnuts, pumpkin seeds, sesame seeds, or flax seeds

Preheat the oven to 300°F. Oil a rimmed baking sheet or jelly-roll pan. In a large bowl, whisk together the sugar, egg white, oil, honey, water, vanilla, and salt until well combined. Stir in the oats, tossing to coat evenly. Spread the oat mixture in an even layer on the pan. Bake for 30 minutes. Stir the granola to redistribute browned bits toward the center of the pan. Reduce the heat to 250°F. Bake for 20 minutes. Stir well again and bake for 20 more minutes. Remove from the oven and stir one final time. Cool completely. Stir in the dried fruit and the nuts/seeds. Store at room temperature in an airtight container.

brunch treats,
coffee cakes,
& quick breads

Plum and Blackberry Kuchen

This lovely, delectable treat is neither a cake nor a tart, but something in between. Baked in a tart pan and piled high with fruit and an almond paste streusel, this spectacular brunch dish is foolproof and easy to prepare. There's no dough to roll out, and the same mixture used for the crust also goes into the streusel topping. Unlike most coffee cakes, it's still moist the next day. The richness of almond paste is the perfect foil for tart berries. I offer two variations so that you may enjoy it year-round with in-season fruit.

MAKES 8 SERVINGS.

½ C. unsalted butter, soft
⅓ C. almond paste
½ C. plus 1 Tbs. sugar (divided)
1¼ C. all-purpose flour
1 tsp. baking powder
½ tsp. ground ginger
¼ tsp. ground cinnamon
¼ tsp. salt

1 C. blackberries
3 medium red plums, sliced
2 Tbs. brandy or amaretto
⅓ C. toasted sliced almonds
⅓ C. half-and-half
1 large egg
1 tsp. vanilla extract
¼ tsp. almond extract

Preheat the oven to 375°F with a large baking sheet on the center rack. Lightly butter a 9½"-round tart pan with a removable bottom. In a medium bowl, beat the butter, almond paste, and ½ cup sugar until smooth, pressing out any almond paste lumps with the back of the spoon, about 3 minutes. (If the almond paste is hard and dry, try grating on the large holes of a box grater directly into the bowl and then creaming as directed.) Dump the flour over the creamed mixture and then sprinkle the baking powder, ginger, cinnamon, and salt on top of the flour. Stir until the mixture almost comes together. (It will look a little shaggy.)

Lightly press two-thirds of this mixture (about 2 cups) into the bottom of the tart pan. Combine the chosen fruit mixture with the brandy or amaretto. Spoon the fruit mixture over the dough in the pan. Crumble the sliced almonds with your fingers over the remaining dough (about 1 cup); toss to combine. Break the dough into small pieces and sprinkle over the fruit. Place the tart pan on the baking sheet and bake for 15 minutes.

Meanwhile, whisk together the half-and-half, egg, vanilla, and almond extract. After the first 15 minutes of baking time, pour this mixture over the coffee cake; then sprinkle remaining tablespoon of sugar over the top. Bake for another 25 to 30 minutes or until the center is set and a knife inserted into the center comes out clean. Cool the pan on a wire rack for 30 minutes before serving.

→ **PEAR AND CRANBERRY KUCHEN:** Use 2 small pears, peeled, cored, and chopped into ½" pieces instead of the plums, and 1 cup cranberries, coarsely chopped, in place of the blackberries.

Blueberry Crumb Cake

Mildly spiced and topped with a delicate streusel, this tender cake barely holds together to make it into your mouth, falling apart as that first warm bite passes your lips. It's great warm for breakfast, and it packs up nicely for a wonderful picnic or lunch-box treat. Other berries will work, too; increase the sugar slightly if you use very tart fruit. You can make crumb cake all year round thanks to frozen berries; just be sure to fully thaw and drain them on paper towels first.

MAKES 9 SERVINGS.

1½ C. all-purpose flour
¾ C. sugar (divided)
1 tsp. baking powder
¼ plus ⅛ tsp. salt
¼ tsp. baking soda
½ C. plus 1 Tbs. unsalted butter
   (divided)

½ C. sour cream
1 large egg
1 tsp. vanilla extract
⅛ tsp. ground cinnamon
⅛ tsp. ground allspice
⅛ tsp. freshly grated nutmeg
1½ C. blueberries

Preheat the oven to 375°F. Butter a 9"-square pan. In a medium bowl, whisk together the flour, ½ cup plus 2 tablespoons of the sugar, the baking powder, salt, and baking soda. Using a pastry blender or your fingers, cut ½ cup butter into the flour mixture until well combined—most of the butter pieces will be smaller than the size of a pea.

For the crumb topping, transfer ¾ cup of the butter-flour mixture to a small bowl. To this, add the remaining 2 tablespoons sugar and the remaining tablespoon butter. Using your fingers, work the butter into the flour mixture until the mixture clumps slightly when pressed.

In a small bowl, whisk together the sour cream, egg, and vanilla. Add the spices to the remaining flour mixture (the non–crumb topping part) and stir to combine. Toss the blueberries with the mixture. Gently fold in the sour cream mixture, stirring just until the batter is combined. The batter will be thick.

Spread the batter evenly in the pan. Sprinkle the reserved crumb mixture over the top, using your fingers to press some of the topping into clumps. Bake for 30 minutes, until a wooden skewer inserted into the middle comes out clean. Cool the cake in the pan set on a wire rack for 15 to 20 minutes—it will be too tender to handle at first. Cut into squares and serve.

Sour Cream Crumb Cake

This recipe comes to me from ex–pastry chef Lisa Bell. She likes to add fresh or frozen berries to the batter and cinnamon to the streusel. I offer this plain version, which lets the flavors of butter and sour cream shine, but I encourage you to add your own creative twists—a white sugar streusel rather than a brown sugar streusel, the addition of your favorite spices (cardamom is quite nice) to the cake batter, adding up to ¼ cup chopped nuts to the streusel, or, of course, adding your favorite fruit to the cake (cranberries, pears, or blueberries are excellent).

MAKES 15 SQUARES.

CAKE

2½ C. cake flour
2 tsp. baking powder
¼ tsp. baking soda
¾ tsp. salt
1 C. unsalted butter, soft

1½ C. sugar
3 large eggs, at room temperature
2 tsp. vanilla extract
1 C. sour cream, at room temperature

STREUSEL

⅔ C. all-purpose flour
½ C. packed light brown sugar

Pinch of salt
¼ C. unsalted butter, soft

Preheat the oven to 350°F. Butter and flour a 13" x 9" baking pan. For the cake, in a small bowl, whisk together the cake flour, baking powder, baking soda, and salt; set aside. In a large bowl, beat the butter and sugar until light and fluffy, 2 to 3 minutes. One at a time, beat in the eggs and then the vanilla extract. Beat in the flour mixture and sour cream alternately until just combined, ending with the flour. Spread the batter evenly in the pan.

For the streusel, in a small bowl, stir together the flour, sugar, and salt. Using your fingers, work the butter into the flour mixture until mixture begins to clump. Sprinkle the streusel evenly over the batter. Bake the cake in the center of the oven for 35 to 40 minutes or until a wooden skewer inserted into the center comes out clean. Cool the cake in the pan set on a wire rack for 15 to 20 minutes. Cut into squares and serve while still warm.

Cream Scones

A perfect cream scone is a thing of beauty. Sadly, most coffee shops and bakeries offer dry, crumbly shadows of what could be, so it's up to you to make your own. I can't resist them, and thanks to Michael Henry, coffee-shop proprietor extraordinaire, I now make killer cream scones. His scones have the loveliest texture—a nice, moist crumb, not too dry, not too wet—just right! Overmixing and too much handling can make for tough, dense scones, but even though Michael considers himself a cook first and baker second, he has a very light touch. I adore plain scones served with a side of preserves, but the recipe is easy to vary. Try adding ⅓ cup dried blueberries and 1 teaspoon lemon zest, for example, or dried cranberries and orange zest. Because scones tend to brown faster on the bottom than the top, I bake them on two baking pans stacked together. To encourage browning on the tops of the scones, I bake them in the upper third of the oven.

MAKES 8 SCONES.

2 C. all-purpose flour
¼ C. sugar
2 tsp. baking powder
¼ tsp. salt
1 tsp. vanilla extract

¾ C. heavy whipping cream plus
   2 Tbs. for brushing
⅓ C. cold unsalted butter, cut
   into ½" pieces
Sugar for sprinkling

Preheat the oven to 375°F. Stack two baking sheets together and line the top one with parchment paper. In a large bowl, whisk together the flour, sugar, baking powder, and salt. Stir the vanilla extract into the heavy cream. With a pastry blender, cut the butter into the flour until a few pea-sized lumps remain. With a fork, gradually stir in enough of the ¾ cup heavy cream until the mixture just starts to come together. Turn the dough out onto a lightly floured surface and very gently pat into an 8" round about 1½" high. Using a chef's knife or bench scraper, cut the dough round into 8 wedges. Transfer the wedges to the baking sheet, spacing the scones at least 1" apart. Brush the tops with the remaining heavy cream and sprinkle liberally with sugar. Bake in the top third of the oven for 15 to 18 minutes or until the tops are golden. Transfer the scones to a wire rack to cool slightly, 3 to 4 minutes. Serve warm with jam.

Brownie Scones

This is my favorite recipe in the book, my beloved comfort snack of choice. Yes, it's a scone, with wonderful crunchy edges, but the inside is moist and rich, like a brownie. You'll need a tall glass of milk after eating just one. Unlike most scones, chocolate scones benefit from the handling or kneading of the dough—without it, they tend to lose their shape in the oven. Be careful not to overbake them—the inside should be just a touch underdone when you pull them from the oven, as the crumb will continue to set as the scones cool.

MAKES 8 SCONES.

4 oz. unsweetened chocolate, coarsely chopped
1 C. all-purpose flour
1 C. cake flour
⅔ C. sugar
¼ C. unsweetened cocoa powder
1 Tbs. baking powder
¼ plus ⅛ tsp. salt
1 large egg

⅓ C. plus 2 Tbs. heavy whipping cream (divided)
2 tsp. molasses
1 tsp. vanilla extract
7 Tbs. cold unsalted butter
1 (3.5 oz.) bar semisweet or bittersweet chocolate, finely chopped
Sugar for sprinkling

In a bowl set over simmering water, melt the unsweetened chocolate; set aside in a warm place so that the chocolate stays melted. Meanwhile, in a large bowl, whisk together the flours, sugar, cocoa powder, baking powder, and salt until well combined. In another small bowl, whisk together the egg, ⅓ cup of heavy cream, molasses, and vanilla; set aside. With a pastry blender, cut the cold butter into the dry ingredients until a few pea-sized lumps remain. First drizzle the cream-egg mixture over the dry ingredient–butter mixture, and then drizzle in the melted unsweetened chocolate. With a fork, stir until the mixture just barely starts to clump together. Lightly mix in the chopped semisweet chocolate. There will still be a few bits of unincorporated dry ingredients at the bottom of the bowl. It's okay—don't keep mixing past this point.

Preheat the oven to 375°F. Line a baking sheet with parchment paper. Turn the dough and any dry bits out onto a lightly floured surface and divide the mass in half. With floured hands, form the two pieces of dough into two 5" squares about 1½" high. (It's okay to gently work the dough a bit to form into a nice square, tucking the rough edges under. This will actually help make a nice, tall scone with defined edges rather than a blob.) With a bench scraper or chef's knife, cut each square on the diagonal into four triangles. Place the triangles on the baking sheet, at least 1" apart. Brush the tops with remaining 2 tablespoons of heavy cream and sprinkle with sugar. Bake for 14 to 16 minutes or until the cut sides of the scones look just set. (Don't overbake, since the scones will continue to set up on the hot baking sheet.) Cool the scones on the baking sheet until just firm enough to move, 2 to 3 minutes. Transfer the scones to a wire rack and cool for 3 to 4 minutes.

Almond Paste Scones

Almond paste gives these scones a sophisticated, grown-up flair. They can be dressed up by stirring in amaretto-soaked dried cherries (and even some chopped white chocolate), or dressed down with mini chocolate chips. Either way, they're delicious.

MAKES 8 SCONES.

2 C. all-purpose flour
2 Tbs. sugar
2 tsp. baking powder
¼ plus ⅛ tsp. salt
⅓ C. packed almond paste
⅓ C. cold unsalted butter
⅓ C. dried cherries* or ⅓ C. mini
  semisweet chocolate chips

⅓ C. heavy whipping cream or
  half-and-half
1 large egg
½ tsp. vanilla extract
¼ tsp. almond extract
Sugar for sprinkling

Preheat the oven to 375°F. Stack two baking sheets together and line the top one with parchment paper. In a large bowl, whisk together the flour, sugar, baking powder, and salt. Using the large holes on a box grater, grate the almond paste and then the butter directly into the dry ingredients. With a pastry blender, cut the almond paste and the butter into the dry ingredients until a few pea-sized lumps remain. Stir in the cherries or mini chocolate chips. In a separate small bowl, whisk together the heavy cream, egg, and extracts. With a fork, gradually stir in enough of the liquid until the mixture just starts to come together, reserving about 1 tablespoon of the liquid to brush the tops of the scones. Turn the dough out onto a lightly floured surface and very gently pat into an 8" round about 1½" high. Using a chef's knife or bench scraper, cut the dough round into 8 wedges. Transfer the wedges to the baking sheet, spacing the scones at least 1" apart. Lightly brush the tops of the scones with the reserved egg-cream mixture and sprinkle liberally with sugar. Bake in the top third of the oven for 15 to 18 minutes or until the tops are golden. Transfer the scones to a wire rack to cool slightly, 3 to 4 minutes. Serve warm.

*NOTE: If your dried fruit is not moist, try heating it in a bit of juice or liqueur to make it more tender and flavorful.

Zucchini Bread

This is a delicious way to eat zucchini. During my childhood "I hate vegetables" years I ate tons of this, never figuring out that within this moist cake lurked a fair amount of vegetable matter (very clever, Mom!). I like it cold, with a soft cream cheese spread, but it is especially tender at room temperature. You can use a light olive oil in place of the oil for a nice variation.

MAKES 10 SERVINGS.

2 C. grated zucchini
¾ C. oil
⅔ C. sugar
⅔ C. packed brown sugar
3 large eggs
1 Tbs. grated lemon zest
1 Tbs. fresh lemon juice
2 C. all-purpose flour
2 tsp. baking powder

¾ tsp. salt
½ tsp. baking soda
½ tsp. ground cinnamon
¼ tsp. freshly grated nutmeg
⅛ tsp. or a hearty pinch of
   ground cloves
¾ C. lightly toasted chopped
   walnuts

Preheat the oven to 350°F. Butter and flour a 9" x 5" loaf pan. With a good deal of enthusiasm, vigorously squeeze as much water out of the grated zucchini as possible; reserve. In a large bowl, whisk together the oil, sugars, eggs, lemon zest, and lemon juice until reasonably light and fluffy, 1 to 2 minutes. Stir in the reserved zucchini. In a medium bowl, whisk together the flour, baking powder, salt, baking soda, cinnamon, nutmeg, and cloves until well combined. Dump the flour mixture into the bowl and sprinkle the walnuts over the flour. Gently fold the dry ingredients into the wet ingredients until the batter just barely comes together. (A silicone spatula works great for this because you can fold the batter up and over easily without overmixing the batter.) Scrape the batter into the pan and level with a good rap on the counter. Bake for 50 to 60 minutes or until a skewer inserted near the center comes out with only moist crumbs clinging. Cool in the pan on a wire rack for 15 minutes. Cool completely out of the pan on the wire rack.

Coconut Banana Bread

Because overripe bananas plague every kitchen, more than one kind of banana bread is necessary. Banana bread is something to get adventurous with. A friend of mine pairs crystallized ginger with banana, which is wonderful (you'd need about ¼ cup finely minced crystallized ginger per loaf). I've seen recipes that combine pumpkin and banana to make moist, flavorful bread. Here, coconut, toasted pecans, and the perky brightness of lemon zest combine for an intriguing version of traditional banana bread. I've used oil instead of butter because it makes a softer loaf, especially if the bread is kept in the refrigerator. I have no idea why I keep it in the refrigerator, except that it's easy to spread butter or sweetened cream cheese on it when it's cold, and it's just plain good that way.

MAKES 10 SERVINGS.

1¼ C. mashed bananas (about 2 large)

1 C. sugar

½ C. oil

2 large eggs

¼ C. buttermilk or sour cream

1 Tbs. grated lemon zest

2 C. all-purpose flour

2 tsp. baking powder

½ tsp. baking soda

¼ plus ⅛ tsp. salt

½ C. packed sweetened flaked coconut

½ C. toasted chopped pecans

Preheat the oven to 350°F. Butter and flour a 9" x 5" loaf pan. In a large bowl, whisk together the bananas, sugar, oil, eggs, buttermilk or sour cream, and lemon zest until reasonably light and fluffy, 1 to 2 minutes. In a medium bowl, whisk together the flour, baking powder, baking soda, and salt until well combined. Dump the flour mixture into the bowl and sprinkle the coconut and pecans over the flour. Gently fold the dry ingredients into the wet ingredients until the batter just barely comes together. (A silicone spatula works great for this because you can fold the batter up and over easily without overmixing the batter.) Scrape the batter into the pan and level with a good rap on the counter. Bake for 45 to 50 minutes or until a skewer inserted near the center comes out with only moist crumbs clinging. Cool in the pan on a wire rack for 15 minutes. Cool completely out of the pan on the wire rack.

→ **CHOCOLATE BANANA BREAD**: Omit the lemon, coconut, and pecans. Substitute ⅓ cup unsweetened cocoa for ⅓ cup of the flour. Stir in ½ cup mini chocolate chips.

Sweet Corn Cake

I love corn bread, but not the dry kind. Corn bread to me should be fluffy, just a touch sweet, and moist with fresh, tender corn. You can make this recipe savory by reducing the sugar to 3 tablespoons and adding grated cheddar or Monterey Jack cheese and chopped serrano or jalapeño chiles. (Add these ingredients with the fresh corn.) For this recipe it's especially important to have your buttermilk at room temperature, or the butter will solidify into little clumps and the texture of the cake will not be as nice.

MAKES 8 SERVINGS.

1 C. buttermilk, at room temperature
6 Tbs. unsalted butter, melted
1 large egg, at room temperature
1 C. fresh corn kernels
1 C. all-purpose flour
½ C. cake flour

½ C. fine-ground yellow cornmeal
⅓ C. sugar
2 tsp. baking powder
½ tsp. baking soda
½ tsp. salt

Preheat the oven to 350°F. Butter and flour either an 8" (at least 2" high) or a standard 9"-round cake pan. In a medium bowl, whisk together the buttermilk, melted butter, and the egg until well combined. Stir in the corn kernels. In another medium bowl, whisk together the flours, cornmeal, sugar, baking powder, baking soda, and salt until well combined. Gently fold the dry ingredients into the wet ingredients until the batter just barely comes together. (A silicone spatula works great for this because you can fold the batter up and over easily without overmixing the batter.) Scrape the batter into the pan and smooth the top with an offset spatula. Bake for 25 to 30 minutes or until a skewer inserted near the center comes out with only moist crumbs clinging. Cool in the pan on a wire rack for 15 minutes.

yeast breads

While cookies and cakes are pretty straightforward, with yeast breads a little upfront information about ingredients and technique can save you both time and effort. For some technical information about yeast and what makes it happy, see page 19 in the ingredient section in Chapter 1. I am including the primer on kneading right here . . . where you "knead" it. (Sorry, couldn't help myself.) Since making bread at home has fallen out of favor over the past 30 years, you may not have had the opportunity to watch anyone make bread. Watching somebody knead and seeing what a properly kneaded dough looks and feels like is the easiest way to learn, but honestly, it's not that difficult. Reading through this section before you make any of the recipes will enable you to make great bread on the first attempt. If you have some idea of what is actually happening when you knead, that understanding will help you achieve better bread. If I can do it, you can do it.

Kneading Know-How

WHAT DOES KNEADING REALLY DO, ANYWAY?

Kneading develops the protein in the dough, providing the structure that makes for a fine-textured loaf of bread that is both soft and pleasantly chewy (rather than cakey and crumbly). Flour contains a protein called glutenin, and when glutenin comes in contact with water (or any water-containing liquid, such as milk), the protein gluten is formed in the dough. The strands of gluten are pretty unorganized at first, but as the dough is kneaded, and even as it rests, they start to align into a neater network. If there has been enough kneading (if the gluten has been "developed," in baker lingo), this network is strong enough to trap the bubbles of carbon dioxide released by the yeast. Then, in the intense heat of the oven, those little gas cells will expand, still trapped in the protein network, and make the dough rise dramatically in the beginning of the baking process.

THIS SOUNDS LIKE A LOT OF TROUBLE—IS ALL THAT KNEADING REALLY NECESSARY?

That depends on how much of hurry you're in. If you can wait over 24 hours, you won't really need to knead much at all. It turns out that if you are just patient—really, really patient—those gluten strands will organize themselves into a strong network without the use of brute force. Unfortunately, most of us are in a hurry, which means it's time to give your upper arms a workout.

ARE THERE ANY SHORTCUTS?

Artisan bakers use what is called an autolyse step to get a jump on gluten development. You mix some of the flour with all of the yeast and water and simply let it sit for 20 to 30 minutes. An autolyse is great for two reasons. One, this gives the yeast a head start, since it works fastest in a soft dough of just flour and water. This jump start is especially important in doughs that will have a lot of sugar and fat, because those ingredients make the yeast sluggish.

And, as for the second benefit, in doughs without an autolyse, the gluten may not actually be getting much development during the first few minutes of kneading. Why? The protein in the flour must come into contact with water to make gluten, so it's possible that the flour is still hydrating for the first few minutes of kneading. And since maximum gluten development can't occur until the flour has fully absorbed all the water, it's really a more efficient use of your time and effort to just wait. The second benefit of the autolyse is that after their peaceful little rest, the gluten proteins start to organize all by themselves, reducing your actual kneading time.

SO HOW DO YOU TELL WHEN THE GLUTEN HAS BEEN DEVELOPED?
Most books say to knead until the dough is soft, smooth, and elastic. While this is true, don't be tempted to shortcut the process by adding more than a tablespoon or two of flour to the board as you knead, or you'll end up with bread that seems dry and stale. The best test of gluten development is to pinch and stretch a piece of dough between your fingers, trying to make a translucent sheet out of it—this is called a gluten window. Even the faintest hint of one is a surefire sign that you've done your job and your finished bread will have a fine-textured, silky, and resilient crumb. The caveat? It takes 12 to 15 minutes of kneading to get there, depending on your style.

IS THERE AN EASY WAY TO KNEAD FOR FOLKS WHO AREN'T SO ENERGETIC?
Why, yes, I have perfected my own lazy kneading method. First of all, I knead on a wooden cutting board or pie board. Wood requires less flour to prevent sticking than any other material. Off to the side I portion out my allotted kneading flour, usually 2 to 3 tablespoons. I'll rub the tiniest bit of flour into the board periodically, meting out flour as if I were the stingiest person on earth. I dump the sticky dough onto the board, and with lightly floured hands and my trusty bench scraper, I fold the dough over onto itself until it forms a ball. Then the real work begins. I usually lean on my left elbow and use my right hand to fold the dough over toward me, then push it back with the heel of my hand. When the dough sticks, I use the bench scraper to scrape it off. I knead this way until I am tired, then I switch arms. If I get very tired, or the dough is very sticky, I cover it and walk away for a few minutes—remember, the gluten is still doing something, even if I'm not. Alternating arms and leaning on one elbow will help you to make it though a kneading marathon.

Basic Sweet Dough

I'd been making good cinnamon rolls for many years, but they got better when my very smart boss (PhD in cereal-grain chemistry kind of smart), Bernie Bruinsma, convinced me to use a simple white-bread dough with added butter as my basic sweet-roll dough. He was right—the texture improved when I took out the egg that had been in my previous recipe, and with the added butter, the richness of milk I'd always included wasn't necessary.

There are two keys to making bread with a texture so perfect that you'll get tears in your eyes. One is properly developing the protein structure of the dough through both kneading and resting periods (see page 72). The second has to do with keeping the water-flour ratio just right, which for you means resisting at all costs the desire to knead more and more flour into the dough. The dough will naturally smooth out and become less sticky as it is worked, and adding too much flour will make the crumb of the finished rolls dry and seemingly stale.

Cinnamon Rolls, Overnight Cinnamon Rolls, Caramel-Pecan Sticky Buns, and Doughnuts (recipes follow) are all made with the Basic Sweet Dough recipe— with options as far as timing, fillings, and even how the dough is cooked—but still it's just one easy basic recipe to learn.

3 C. all-purpose flour (divided)	¼ C. unsalted butter, melted
1 (¼-oz.) pkg. fast-acting yeast	3 Tbs. sugar
1 C. very warm water (115°F)	1¼ tsp. salt

In a medium bowl, combine half the flour with the yeast. Stir in the warm water until combined. Cover the bowl and let ferment in a warm spot in your kitchen for 30 minutes. Stir the melted butter, sugar, and salt into the bubbly sponge. Stir in the remaining flour as best you can to make a stiff, shaggy dough. Turn the dough out onto a lightly floured wooden board and begin to knead.

As you knead, sprinkle only tiny amounts of extra flour onto the board to prevent the dough from sticking. Rely on your bench scraper at the beginning of kneading to fold the dough over itself, since it will be quite sticky. Do not add more than a total of 2 to 3 tablespoons of flour during the 10 minutes of kneading. Extra flour will make the finished rolls dry, tough, and seemingly stale. As you continue to knead, the dough will smooth out and become very easy to handle. Knead for as long as you can stand it—this is what will give your bread great texture. Ideally, you should be able to pinch the end of the dough and stretch it into a thin, translucent sheet. Place the dough in a lightly buttered mixing bowl, cover with plastic wrap, and let rise in a warm place until doubled in bulk, about 30 minutes. At this point, see specific recipes that follow for further instructions.

Cinnamon Rolls

There is nothing, nothing like a homemade cinnamon roll. My boss's family (the aforementioned PhD Bernie) is so crazy about them that they even serve them with Thanksgiving dinner! See the Overnight Cinnamon Rolls variation at the end of the recipe if you know you won't have time in the morning to make these straight through.

MAKES 9 GOOD-SIZED ROLLS.

1 recipe Basic Sweet Dough (page 74; prepared through the first rise stage)

3 Tbs. unsalted butter, soft
⅓ C. packed brown sugar
2 tsp. ground cinnamon

GLAZE

3 Tbs. cream cheese, very soft
1 tsp. vanilla extract

Pinch salt
1 C. powdered sugar

Gently press out excess air from the risen Basic Sweet Dough. Turn the dough out onto a lightly floured wooden board and shape into a rectangle. Roll into a 14" x 11" rectangle. Using an offset spatula, spread 2 to 3 table-spoons of the soft butter evenly over the dough to within ⅛" of the edge. Combine the brown sugar with the cinnamon in a small bowl; sprinkle the mixture evenly over the butter, spreading it with your fingers if necessary.

Roll up the dough lengthwise, starting to roll from the long edge. Pinch the seam to seal. Roll the log on the board so that it's seam side down. With a ser-rated knife, gently trim ½" off each end. Cut the log into thirds and then cut each third into three slices. Arrange the slices evenly in a buttered 9"-square pan, cut side down. Cover the pan with plastic wrap and let the rolls rise in a warm spot until doubled in volume, about 30 minutes.

Preheat the oven to 375°F. Bake the rolls for 24 to 28 minutes, until the tops and edges are browned and the rolls near the center of the pan are no longer doughy. Meanwhile, for the glaze, in a small bowl, beat the cream cheese with the vanilla and salt until smooth. Gradually beat in the powdered sugar until no lumps remain. When the rolls come out of the oven, spread evenly with the glaze.

→ **OVERNIGHT CINNAMON ROLLS:** Overnight rolls are perfect for folks who don't have a lot of time in the morning. As a bonus, the long, cool fermentation makes for wonderfully flavorful rolls. For Overnight Cinnamon Rolls, prepare the Cinnamon Roll recipe as directed, except reduce the yeast by ¾ teaspoon. Let the dough rise on the counter, then roll, fill, slice, and place in the pan, as directed in the recipe. Cover with plastic wrap and refrigerate overnight. Let the cinnamon rolls rise the next morning at room temperature until doubled, and bake as directed. Note that both the initial rise and the rise of the shaped rolls will take a bit longer than in the original recipe: the first because there is less yeast present and the second because the dough will be cold at first.

Reducing the amount of yeast prevents the dough from overfermenting as it rises slowly all night in the refrigerator. Since this bread is rich with sugar and fat, the recipe most likely wouldn't fail if you didn't cut the yeast back. However, recipes that are higher in water (yeast works faster in liquid batters) would fail—the yeast would overferment, creating too much alcohol, aldehydes, and ketones. Those flavorful compounds are all great in moderation, but too much of a good thing can make your bread taste unpleasantly "yeasty."

Caramel-Pecan Sticky Buns

Cinnamon rolls are not for everyone. There's a sticky-bun faction that prefers gooey, nut-topped rolls to ordinary cinnamon rolls, and for them I offer this recipe. It's the same dough, rolled the same way, with a totally different topping.

MAKES 9 LARGE STICKY BUNS.

STICKY BUN GOO

1¼ C. sugar

⅓ C. dark corn syrup

1 Tbs. lemon juice

1 tsp. vanilla extract

⅛ tsp. salt

1 C. pecan halves

1 recipe Cinnamon Rolls (page 76; prepared to the point that the rolls are cut and ready to go into the pan)

In a medium bowl, whisk all the Sticky Bun Goo ingredients except the nuts together until smooth. With an offset spatula, spread the goo across the bottom of a well-buttered 9"-square baking pan. Sprinkle the nuts over the goo. Arrange the cinnamon roll slices evenly in the pan over the goo, cut side down. Cover the pan with plastic wrap and let the rolls rise in a warm spot until doubled in volume, about 30 minutes.

Preheat the oven to 375°F. Bake the rolls for 24 to 28 minutes, until the tops and edges are browned and the rolls near the center of the pan are no longer doughy.

Invert the pan onto a serving tray or cookie sheet immediately after removing the buns from the oven to release the caramel and pecans. If the caramel cools, it will be difficult to get the buns out of the pan. Let stand until cool enough to handle, but serve while still warm.

Doughnuts

Every now then, not every day, mind you, but once and a while, it's good to indulge à la Homer Simpson. Mmmmm... doughnuts. And homemade doughnuts are so much better than store-bought that it kind of takes the edge off the guilt. Doughnuts are, of course, the ultimate crowd-pleaser and great to whip up when you are entertaining over the holidays or have houseguests on a snowy winter morning. Everyone will want to help. Okay, maybe it's not an outpouring of pure altruism—it may just be positioning to be in place to get that first warm doughnut—but still, help is help. So, take advantage, set up a glazing station, and let the little ones (or the little ones in big bodies) apply the sprinkles.

MAKES ABOUT 1 DOZEN DOUGHNUTS.

1 recipe Basic Sweet Dough
   (page 74; prepared through
   the first rise stage)
Vegetable oil suitable for frying

Powdered Sugar Glaze, Chocolate
   Glaze (see below), cinnamon-
   sugar, or powdered sugar

Deflate the Basic Sweet Dough gently and let rise again in a warm place until doubled. On a lightly floured surface or pie board, roll out the dough to a ¾" thickness. Using a 2½" to 3" doughnut cutter, cut out the doughnuts. Reroll the scraps and cut out more doughnuts. In a cast-iron skillet, pour in enough oil to come 1" up the side of the pan. Heat the oil to 365°F over medium-high heat. Fry the doughnuts in batches until golden, turning once, about 2 minutes per side. Take care not to crowd the pan in order to maintain a steady frying temperature—the temperature will drop every time doughnuts are added to the oil. Drain the cooked doughnuts on paper towels briefly, then top with Powdered Sugar Glaze or Chocolate Glaze, or simply dust with cinnamon-sugar or powdered sugar.

POWDERED SUGAR GLAZE

4 to 6 Tbs. milk or water
1 tsp. vanilla extract

½ C. powdered sugar

In a small bowl, gradually whisk the liquids into the powdered sugar until the glaze is thin enough to evenly coat the top of a cooked doughnut when it is dipped into the glaze. Add more liquid to thin the glaze or more sugar to thicken it as needed.

CHOCOLATE GLAZE

1 (3.5 oz.) bar bittersweet chocolate, chopped

⅓ C. corn syrup (light or dark)

2 Tbs. unsalted butter

¼ C. hot water

1 C. powdered sugar

In a small pan set over medium-low heat, melt the chocolate, corn syrup, and butter, stirring occasionally, until smooth. Whisk in the hot water and then the powdered sugar until smooth. Transfer the mixture to a shallow bowl for dipping the tops of the warm doughnuts, or simply drizzle the glaze over the doughnuts with a small spoon.

Monkey Bread

Most monkey bread is simply a variation of cinnamon rolls: pieces of bread dough dipped in butter, rolled in cinnamon-sugar, then stacked in a Bundt pan to rise. After baking, the finished bread is inverted onto a platter, where everyone can dig in and pull apart pieces of bread like monkeys. To give the bread some character, and make it reflect its namesake, I've added banana and mini chocolate chips to the dough. The result is a crowd-pleaser for kids and adults alike. If you have little ones, they'll want to help make this dish.

MAKES 8 SERVINGS.

DOUGH

3 C. all-purpose flour (divided)

1 (¼-oz.) pkg. fast-acting yeast

⅔ C. very warm water (115°F)

1 small to medium ripe banana,
   mashed (⅓ to ½ C.)

¼ C. unsalted butter, melted

3 Tbs. sugar

1½ tsp. salt

In a medium bowl, combine 1 cup of the flour with the yeast. Stir in the warm water until combined. Cover the bowl and let ferment in a warm spot in your kitchen for 20 to 30 minutes. Stir the mashed banana, melted butter, sugar, and salt into the bubbly sponge. Stir in the remaining flour as best you can to make a stiff, shaggy dough. Turn the dough out onto a lightly floured wooden board and begin to knead.

As you knead, sprinkle only tiny amounts of extra flour onto the board to prevent the dough from sticking. Rely on your bench scraper at the beginning of kneading to fold the dough over itself, since it will be quite sticky. Do not add more than a total of 2 to 3 tablespoons of flour during the 10 minutes of kneading. Extra flour will make the finished bread dry, tough, and seemingly stale. As you continue to knead, the dough will smooth out and become very easy to handle. Knead for as long as you can stand it—this is what will give your bread great texture. Ideally, you should be able to pinch the end of the dough and stretch it into a thin, translucent sheet. Place the dough in a lightly buttered mixing bowl, cover with plastic wrap, and let rise in a warm place until doubled in bulk, about 30 minutes.

FILLING

⅔ C. sugar

1 Tbs. ground cinnamon

¼ C. unsalted butter, melted

¼ C. mini semisweet chocolate chips

Liberally butter a 12-cup Bundt pan. In a small bowl, combine the sugar and cinnamon; set aside. Pour the melted butter into another small bowl. Gently press out the excess air in the dough and turn it out onto a lightly floured wooden board. Roll into a 14" x 9" rectangle. Brush lightly with about 1 tablespoon of the melted butter. Sprinkle with the mini chocolate chips and then with 1 tablespoon of the cinnamon-sugar.

Roll up the dough lengthwise, starting to roll from the long edge. Pinch the seam to seal. Roll the log on the board so that it's seam side down. With a bench scraper or knife, cut the log in half crosswise. Stretch the small logs to about 8" long. Cut each of these logs lengthwise (into two skinnier 8" logs—you now have four logs), and then cut each log into six pieces. Dip each piece in the remaining melted butter in the bowl and then roll in the remaining cinnamon-sugar. Place the sugared dough balls into the Bundt pan, stacking neatly. Butter the top of the dough. Cover and let rise in a warm place until doubled in bulk, 40 to 50 minutes.

Preheat the oven to 375°F. Bake for 23 to 25 minutes or until a skewer inserted into the middle comes out with only moist crumbs clinging. Let cool briefly in the pan, about 3 minutes. Invert onto a serving platter. Don't wait any longer than 3 minutes to unmold or the bread will stick to the pan.

Delicate Orange-Raisin Morning Rolls

This recipe marries the flavors of French savarin or babas with the texture of a morning bun. The result is a delightful alternative to cinnamon rolls and sticky buns. Cardamom is a cool, fragrant spice that's a refreshing change from warm spices such as allspice and cinnamon, which typically dominate baking. The faint hint of spice complements the orange zest without being assertive. These rolls are the latest weekend favorite at my house.

MAKES 9 GOOD-SIZED ROLLS.

DOUGH

3 C. all-purpose flour (divided)   ¼ C. sugar
1 (¼-oz.) pkg. fast-acting yeast   1¼ tsp. salt
1 C. very warm water (115°F)   1 tsp. grated orange zest
¼ C. unsalted butter, melted   ¼ tsp. ground cardamom
2 large egg yolks

In a medium bowl, combine half the flour with the yeast. Stir in the warm water until combined. Cover the bowl and let ferment in a warm spot in your kitchen for 30 minutes. Stir the melted butter, egg yolks, sugar, salt, orange zest, and cardamom into the bubbly sponge. Stir in the remaining flour as best you can to make a stiff, shaggy dough. Turn the dough out onto a lightly floured wooden board and begin to knead.

As you knead, sprinkle only tiny amounts of extra flour into the board to prevent the dough from sticking. Rely on your bench scraper at the beginning of kneading to fold the dough over itself, since it will be quite sticky. Do not add more than a total of 2 to 3 tablespoons of flour while kneading. Extra flour will make the finished rolls dry, tough, and seemingly stale. As you continue to knead, the dough will smooth out and become very easy to handle. Knead for 10 minutes, or as long as you can stand it—this is what will give your rolls great texture. Ideally, you should be able to pinch the end of the dough and stretch it into a thin, translucent sheet. Place the dough in a lightly buttered mixing bowl, cover with plastic wrap, and let rise in a warm place until doubled in bulk, about 30 minutes.

FILLING

⅔ C. golden raisins   1 Tbs. melted butter
¼ C. dark rum

In a small saucepan, heat the golden raisins and rum over low heat until the raisins just soften, 3 to 4 minutes. Set aside. Gently press out excess air from the dough and turn it out onto a lightly floured wooden board. Roll into a 14" x 11" rectangle. Brush the dough with the melted butter to within ⅛" of the edge. Sprinkle evenly with raisins, draining them if necessary.

Roll up the dough lengthwise, starting to roll from the long edge. Pinch the seam to seal. Roll the log on the board so that it's seam side down. With a serrated knife, gently trim ½" off each end. Cut the log into thirds and then cut each third into three slices. Arrange the slices evenly in a buttered 9"-square pan, cut side down. Cover the pan with plastic wrap and let the rolls rise in a warm spot until doubled in volume, about 30 minutes. Preheat the oven to 375°F. Bake the rolls for 24 to 28 minutes, until the tops and edges are browned and the rolls near the center of the pan are no longer doughy.

GLAZE

1 C. powdered sugar   ½ tsp. vanilla extract
1 Tbs. dark rum   1 to 2 Tbs. fresh orange juice

Meanwhile, for the glaze, in a small bowl, whisk together the powdered sugar, rum, vanilla, and enough orange juice to thin the glaze to spreading consistency. When the rolls come out of the oven, spread evenly with the glaze.

Coffee Cake with Chocolate Streusel

For some reason, it seems that yeasted coffee cakes that were common in my grandmother's era are now out of fashion, and I think that's just too bad. A yeasted coffee cake has a lot to offer: It's not too sweet and it is, literally, great with a cup of coffee. The chocolate streusel is an unusual addition and can be used to top other cakes, like the Sour Cream Crumb Cake (just double it) on page 60 or the Banana Snack Cake on page 150, or even atop your favorite cupcake or muffin recipe. I've also included a Berry Jam and Almond Streusel variation for those of you who prefer something a bit more traditional. That "coffee" cake is actually fabulous with tea.

MAKES 8 SERVINGS.

COFFEE CAKE

1½ C. all-purpose flour (divided)	¼ C. sugar
1 (¼-oz.) pkg. fast-acting yeast	¼ cup unsalted butter, melted
½ C. very warm water (115°F)	¼ tsp. plus ⅛ tsp. salt
2 large egg yolks	

Butter a 9"-round cake pan. In a medium bowl, stir ½ cup of the flour with the yeast to combine. Stir in the warm water. Cover and let sit in a warm place for about 20 minutes. Meanwhile, in a small bowl, stir together the egg yolks, sugar, melted butter, and salt until well combined. Whisk the egg mixture into the sponge until the lumps smooth out. Dump the remaining flour over the sponge. Stir vigorously until the dough starts to come together. Let the dough stand for 10 minutes. Scrape the dough out onto a lightly floured surface (it will be very sticky). Knead, adding up to 3 tablespoons additional flour and turning the dough over on itself with a bench scraper, for at least 4 to 5 minutes. It will still be sticky; don't be alarmed. Scrape the dough into the pan and spread out to the edges with an offset spatula. Cover and let rise in a warm place until halfway up the side of the pan, about 1 hour.

CHOCOLATE STREUSEL

½ C. packed light brown sugar	½ C. chopped nuts, such as almonds,
¼ C. all-purpose flour	walnuts, or pecans (optional)
3 Tbs. unsweetened natural cocoa	¼ tsp. ground cinnamon (optional)
powder	¼ cup unsalted butter, soft
⅛ tsp. salt	

Meanwhile, preheat the oven to 375°F and make the Chocolate Streusel. In a small bowl, stir together the sugar, flour, cocoa powder, and salt until well combined. If desired, stir in the nuts and cinnamon. With your fingers, work the soft butter into the dry mixture until it clumps together when squeezed. Gently sprinkle the streusel over the risen coffee cake and bake for 22 to 25 minutes or until a skewer inserted in the center comes out with fluffy crumbs clinging. Cool in the pan on a wire rack for 15 to 20 minutes. Serve warm.

→ BERRY JAM AND ALMOND STREUSEL COFFEE CAKE

½ C. all-purpose flour
¼ C. packed dark brown sugar
2 Tbs. toasted sliced almonds
⅛ tsp. salt

3 Tbs. unsalted butter, soft
¼ cup tart preserves (cherry, raspberry, or blackberry)

Prepare the Coffee Cake, but don't make the Chocolate Streusel. Instead, as the coffee cake is rising, prepare the Almond Streusel. In a small bowl, stir together the flour, brown sugar, almonds, and salt until well combined. With your fingers, work the soft butter into the dry mixture until it clumps together when squeezed. Gently dot the preserves over the risen coffee cake by the teaspoonful. Sprinkle with the streusel. Bake, cool, and serve as directed.

Overnight Yeast-Raised Waffles

Yeast-raised waffles are like no other kind: Airy, delicate, and super-crisp, they have a complex, almost sourdough-like flavor that comes from a long, slow fermentation. The batter sits out on the counter all night and is ready to go first thing in the morning. Recipes abound for yeast-raised waffles, but few are as good as the one Marion Cunningham published nearly 30 years ago. This is a modern version of hers, using instant yeast (also known as quick- or fast-rising yeast) instead of active dry yeast. Instant yeast does best when combined directly with the flour, thus eliminating the need to proof the yeast in warm water. Because fresh milk contains enzymes that inhibit the yeast, the milk must first be scalded to eliminate them. Don't worry about leaving a batter containing milk out all night—you've already sterilized it, and besides, if you're lucky the batter will have the pleasant tang of buttermilk by morning.

MAKES 12 TO 14 STANDARD WAFFLES.

2½ C. milk	1 tsp. sugar
½ C. unsalted butter	½ tsp. salt
2 C. all-purpose flour	2 large eggs, at room temperature
1½ tsp. fast-acting yeast	½ tsp. baking soda

In a small saucepan, bring the milk to a boil over medium-high heat. Turn off the heat and stir in the butter until melted and smooth. Let the milk mixture cool to very warm, about 115°F. In a large bowl, whisk together the flour, yeast, sugar, and salt. Stir the milk mixture into the flour until well combined. Cover the bowl loosely with plastic wrap, so that air can escape, and leave on the counter overnight, for at least 6 hours but no longer than 10 hours.

The next morning, whisk the eggs and baking soda together in a small bowl. Whisk the eggs gently into the waffle mix. Cook the waffles in a lightly greased, preheated waffle iron according to the manufacturer's instructions. If you no longer have the instructions, follow the old adage that waffles are done when the flow of steam from the iron lessens. This is usually 1½ to 3 minutes, depending on how crisp you like your waffles. Waffles quickly lose their crispy edges, so hold them in a 300°F to 350°F oven, right on the rack.

05

COOKIES
& BARS

Cookies are my weakness, and it was difficult to rein in the number of cookie recipes I wanted to include in this book. You'll notice that there are still more recipes for cookies than for cakes or pies, and I believe that to be justified—most people are more comfortable baking cookies than anything else. Is there anyone who hasn't made chocolate chip cookies from scratch, at least once?

Chewy-Crisp Chocolate Chip Cookies

The quest for the perfect chocolate chip cookie recipe is my Holy Grail. My current favorite yields cookies that are crisp at the edges and chewy in the middle—provided you take the cookies out of the oven in time! There is a bit of shortening in this recipe, which makes a taller, smoother cookie. Rather than wait for the butter to soften on the countertop, I started melting half of it to speed the process along. This technique has the wonderful side effect of making the cookies taste distinctively buttery. For cookies that are sandy and crisp, omit the shortening and use all melted butter. For special occasions, I use a bar of fine-quality bittersweet chocolate, chopped, instead of chocolate chips. Because chocolate chip cookies are best right out of the oven, I suggest baking only a few at a time and keeping the dough on hand in the refrigerator.

MAKES 2½ TO 3 DOZEN COOKIES.

10 Tbs. unsalted butter	2 C. all-purpose flour
2 Tbs. vegetable shortening	¾ tsp. baking soda
⅔ C. sugar	1 C. semisweet chocolate chips
⅔ C. packed dark brown sugar	or chopped bittersweet
1 large egg	chocolate
1 tsp. vanilla extract	1 C. toasted chopped pecans or
½ tsp. salt	walnuts (optional)

Preheat the oven to 350°F. Melt roughly half the butter in a small saucepan; pour the butter into a large bowl. Let stand for 1 minute. Cut the remaining butter into pieces and add to the bowl. Wait 1 minute and add the shortening and both sugars. Beat until fluffy with no lumps, 1 to 2 minutes. Stir in the egg, vanilla, and salt until the dough is smooth and creamy. Stir in the flour and baking soda until almost combined. Add the chocolate and nuts and stir until evenly dispersed.

Line baking sheets with parchment paper and drop walnut-sized chunks of dough (about 2 tablespoons) onto the sheets, spacing at least 1½" apart. Bake the cookies for 11 to 13 minutes, until golden at the edges and puffed in the centers, but not quite set. Let the cookies cool on the baking sheets for 3 minutes before transferring to wire racks to cool completely.

NOTE: For crisp cookies, melt all of the butter in the first step, and bake the cookies until set in the center, 13 to 15 minutes.

Peanut Butter–Molasses Cookies

Here's a cookie for peanut butter lovers to add to their collection. Crisp at the edges and chewy in the middle, this cookie is a cross between a traditional soft molasses cookie and a crisp peanut butter cookie. The marriage of peanut butter and molasses makes for a beguiling eating experience—the peanut butter hits your palate immediately, while the spicy flavor of molasses lingers. Use the best molasses you can find. Barbados-style molasses has a complex flavor characterized by smoke and caramel as well as spicy notes that'll convert even the molasses naysayers.

MAKES 2½ DOZEN COOKIES.

¾ C. unsalted butter, soft
¼ C. creamy peanut butter
1 C. sugar, plus ⅓ cup for rolling
¼ C. dark molasses, preferably
   Barbados style

1 large egg
1 tsp. vanilla extract
½ tsp. salt
2 C. all-purpose flour
1½ tsp. baking soda

Preheat the oven to 375°F. In a large bowl, beat the butter, peanut butter, 1 cup sugar, and molasses until fluffy with no lumps, 1 to 2 minutes. Stir in the egg, vanilla, and salt until the dough is smooth and creamy. Stir in the flour and baking soda until combined.

Line baking sheets with parchment paper. Form walnut-sized balls of dough (about 2 tablespoons) and roll in the remaining sugar. Place the dough balls onto the baking sheets, spacing at least 1½" apart, and flatten slightly. Bake the cookies for 8 to 10 minutes, until golden at the edges and puffed in the centers, but not quite set. Let the cookies cool on the baking sheets for 3 minutes before transferring to wire racks to cool completely.

Chewy-Crisp Drop Sugar Cookies

These crackly-top cookies remind me of trips to the bakery with my grandfather when I was five years old. My fondness for simple sugar cookies has returned, only now I like them without the rainbow sprinkles. These cookies have an intense buttery flavor that comes from barely browning some of the butter, creating an almost nutty flavor. Shortening and corn syrup, respectively, keep the cookies tall and moist. For clean-cut cookies, roll balls of dough in sugar and flatten them slightly with the bottom of a glass before baking. I like rough cookie tops, so I simply drop the dough by the spoonful and sprinkle sanding (large-grain) sugar over the tops before baking.

MAKES 2½ DOZEN COOKIES.

10 Tbs. unsalted butter	1 tsp. vanilla extract
2 Tbs. vegetable shortening	½ tsp. salt
1 C. sugar	2 C. all-purpose flour
1 large egg	¾ tsp. baking soda
1 Tbs. light corn syrup	Sanding sugar for sprinkling (optional)

Preheat the oven to 350°F. Melt roughly half the butter in a small saucepan, bringing it to a boil. Cook the butter for 30 seconds, until it becomes fragrant and pale gold, but don't let it brown. Pour the butter into a large bowl and let it cool for 2 minutes. Cut the remaining butter into pieces and add to the bowl. Wait 1 minute and then add the shortening and sugar to the bowl. Beat until fluffy with no lumps, 1 to 2 minutes. Stir in the egg, corn syrup, vanilla, and salt until the dough is smooth and creamy. Stir in the flour and baking soda until combined.

Line baking sheets with parchment paper and drop walnut-sized chunks of dough (about 2 tablespoons) onto the baking sheets, spacing at least 1½" apart. Sprinkle sanding sugar over the dough chunks. Bake the cookies for 11 to 13 minutes, until golden at the edges and puffed in the centers, but not quite set. Let the cookies cool on the baking sheets for 3 minutes before transferring to wire racks to cool completely.

NOTE: For crisp cookies, melt all of the butter in the first step, and bake the cookies until set in the center, 13 to 15 minutes.

Soft Oatmeal-Raisin Cookies

These thick, chewy cookies stay soft and moist for days, thanks to the addition of water. Many oatmeal cookies are perfect fresh from the oven but tend to become hard and stale within two days. Adding water to the dough and letting the dough sit before it is baked gives the oats time to absorb moisture, which will be retained by the cookies days after they are baked. This recipe is easy on the cinnamon, so feel free to add more if you prefer spicier cookies. Since the cookies are delicate when they first come out of the oven, be sure to let them sit on the pan until they are firm enough to transfer with a spatula. Oh, and if you need further encouragement, the oats, dried fruit, and nuts are packed with both soluble and insoluble fiber, not to mention protein and vitamins—so not only are these cookies delicious, they're also good for you!

MAKES 2½ DOZEN COOKIES.

¾ C. oil

¼ C. water

¾ C. sugar

¾ C. packed dark brown sugar

1 large egg

1 tsp. vanilla extract

1 tsp. salt

1¼ C. all-purpose flour

¾ tsp. baking soda

½ tsp. ground cinnamon

3 C. old-fashioned rolled oats

1 C. raisins, dried cherries, or dried
    sweetened cranberries

1 C. toasted chopped walnuts
    or pecans

¼ C. toasted sesame seeds (optional)

Preheat the oven to 350°F. In a large bowl, beat the oil, water, and sugars until smooth, about 1 minute. Stir in the egg, vanilla, and salt until the dough is creamy. Stir in the flour, baking soda, and cinnamon until almost combined. Stir in the oats, cherries, nuts, and sesame seeds, if desired. Let the dough stand at room temperature for 10 minutes.

Line baking sheets with parchment paper and drop walnut-sized chunks of dough (about 2 tablespoons) onto the baking sheets, spacing at least 1½" apart. Bake the cookies for 11 to 13 minutes, until golden at the edges and puffed in the centers, but not quite set. Let the cookies cool on the baking sheets for 3 minutes before transferring to wire racks to cool completely.

Chewy Peanut Butter–Oatmeal Cookies

When I first tasted the Soft Oatmeal-Raisin Cookies, I thought how wonderful the cookies would be with peanut butter. These cookies have less flour and oats than the previous recipe—peanut butter has a drying, cohesive effect on doughs. You'll have to decide whether to add raisins or chocolate chips, or both, but either way you'll need a tall, cold glass of milk to accompany them.

MAKES 2½ DOZEN COOKIES.

¾ C. oil	1 tsp. vanilla extract
¼ C. water	1 tsp. salt
¾ C. sugar	1 C. plus 2 Tbs. all-purpose flour
¾ C. packed dark brown sugar	½ tsp. baking soda
½ C. creamy peanut butter	2½ C. old-fashioned rolled oats
1 large egg	1 C. raisins and/or 1 C. chocolate chips

Preheat the oven to 350°F. In a large bowl, beat the oil, water, and sugars until smooth, about 1 minute. Beat in the peanut butter until well combined. Stir in the egg, vanilla, and salt until the dough is smooth and creamy. Stir in the flour and baking soda until almost combined. Stir in the oats, raisins, and/or chocolate chips. Let the dough stand at room temperature for 10 minutes.

Line baking sheets with parchment paper and drop walnut-sized chunks of dough (about 2 tablespoons) onto the baking sheets, spacing at least 1½" apart. Bake the cookies for 13 to 14 minutes, until golden at the edges and puffed in the centers, but not quite set. Don't overbake! Let the cookies cool on the baking sheets for 3 minutes before transferring to wire racks to cool completely.

Chocolate Fudge Cookies

These cookies live up to the "fudge" in the title—rich and super-chocolaty. Starting with two good-quality bittersweet candy bars ensures wonderful flavor while making measuring easy. I use Lindt or Valrhona brands, but any chocolate is fine so long as it doesn't exceed 65 percent cocoa solids—more than that and the dough can curdle and will not have enough sugar to spread and be moist. Try baking smaller, bite-sized mini cookies to bring out after a dinner party—they pair well with red wines and port, especially if you add more chopped chocolate or mini chocolate chips to the dough. If you like the contrast of bitter and sweet, stir chopped white chocolate into the dough— anywhere from half to all of a 3.5-ounce bar is good.

MAKES 2 DOZEN COOKIES.

½ C. unsalted butter
2 (3.5-oz.) bars good-quality
   bittersweet chocolate, chopped
1 C. packed light brown sugar
2 large eggs
1 tsp. vanilla extract
¼ tsp. salt

1 C. all-purpose flour
¼ C. unsweetened natural
   cocoa powder
1 tsp. baking powder
1 (3.5-oz.) bar white chocolate,
   preferably Lindt or Rainforest,
   chopped (optional)

Preheat the oven to 350°F. Melt the butter over low heat; add the chopped chocolate and melt completely. Transfer the chocolate-butter mixture to a large bowl; let cool for 5 minutes. Beat in the sugar until fluffy with no lumps, 1 to 2 minutes. Gradually stir in the eggs, vanilla, and salt until smooth and creamy. Stir in the flour, cocoa powder, and baking powder until combined. Stir in the chopped white chocolate, if desired, until evenly dispersed.

Line baking sheets with parchment paper and drop mounds of dough (1½ tablespoons) onto the baking sheets, spacing at least 1½" apart. Bake the cookies for 10 to 12 minutes, until puffed in the centers, but not quite set. Let the cookies cool on the baking sheets for 3 minutes before transferring to wire racks to cool completely.

Anzac Cookies

ANZAC is short for the Australian and New Zealand Army Corps, and these cookies are reputed to have been invented to honor them during WWII. If you haven't heard of them, don't worry—it's not too late to become addicted to these crunchy golden cookies that taste intensely of caramel and butterscotch. The recipe is a good excuse to buy a jar of Lyle's Golden Syrup. There's nothing quite like Lyle's—it's neither bland like corn syrup nor darkly spicy like molasses, nor is it intensely sweet like honey. It's more like a light caramel. Cookies that contain it will brown quickly, much more readily even than cookies with added corn syrup, so check for doneness ahead of the final baking time. Because the cookies brown on the bottom fast, bake them on two baking sheets (aka "double-panning") for better insulation or bake in the upper quadrant of the oven, where the tops will get the greater amount of heat. The cookies may look underdone in the middle, but it is important to take them out of the oven once the edges are golden brown. Don't worry—they'll set up perfectly.

MAKES 2 DOZEN COOKIES.

½ C. unsalted butter, soft	¾ tsp. baking soda
¾ C. sugar	¾ C. old-fashioned rolled oats
2 Tbs. Lyle's Golden Syrup	¾ C. sweetened flaked coconut
½ tsp. salt	¾ C. lightly toasted walnuts,
1 C. all-purpose flour	chopped

Preheat the oven to 350°F. Melt the butter in a medium saucepan and let cool for 1 minute. In the same pan, beat in the sugar, Lyle's Golden Syrup, and salt until smooth. Stir in the flour and baking soda until almost combined. The dough will appear shaggy and sort of mealy—it's okay, don't worry. Stir in the oats, coconut, and walnuts until evenly distributed.

Line baking sheets with parchment paper and place mounds of dough (1½ tablespoons) onto the baking sheets, spacing at least 1½" apart. Press and flatten into disks about ½" high. Bake the cookies for 9 to 10 minutes, until not quite set but browned on the edges. Let the cookies cool on the baking sheets for 5 minutes before transferring to wire racks to cool completely.

Potato Chip Cookies

Potato chips? I know it sounds crazy, but before you skip this recipe, hear me out. If you like pecan sandies or Mexican wedding cakes, you'll like these even better. Yes, I know it sounds ridiculously indulgent to add potato chips to a buttery cookie already studded with toasted pecans, but hey, you only live once. I show up with them at parties all the time, and I never spill the secret ingredient until the plate is empty. Instead, I watch from a distance as folks who say they don't like sweets gobble up every last one. These cookies look quite dainty when sprinkled with powdered sugar, so I get a perverse thrill from watching bourbon-swilling manly-men pop one after another into their mouths.

MAKES 2½ TO 3 DOZEN COOKIES.

1 C. unsalted butter, soft
1 C. powdered sugar
1 large egg yolk
1 tsp. vanilla extract

¼ tsp. salt
1½ C. all-purpose flour
¾ C. finely chopped toasted pecans
¾ C. crushed potato chips

Preheat the oven to 350°F. In a large bowl, beat the butter and powdered sugar until fluffy with no lumps, 1 to 2 minutes. Stir in the egg yolk, vanilla, and salt until the dough is smooth and creamy. Stir in the flour until almost combined. Stir in the pecans until evenly distributed, and then very gently stir in the crushed potato chips.

Line baking sheets with parchment paper and drop dough by the tablespoon onto the baking sheets, spacing at least 1½" apart. Bake the cookies for 11 to 13 minutes, until golden on the edges and set in the middle. Let the cookies cool on the baking sheets for 3 minutes before transferring to wire racks to cool completely.

Brussels-Style Oat Crisps Filled with Chocolate

Thin and super-crisp, these elegant cookies are a treat I make for special occasions and parties. Easy to make and fast to bake, with the actual work quick and simple, these cookies belie their polished appearance. I have a peanut butter addiction, so my favorite way to eat them is with the thin layer of peanut butter filling, below, but they are equally tasty with the chocolate filling. Don't fill the cookies with the peanut butter filling until just before serving. The chocolate-filled cookies, on the other hand, can be assembled ahead of time and held at room temperature. The unfilled cookies are lovely plain with ice cream.

MAKES ABOUT 100 CRISPS OR 50 SANDWICH COOKIES.

½ C. unsalted butter
1 C. sugar
1 large egg
½ tsp. salt

¾ C. plus 2 Tbs. all-purpose flour
½ tsp. baking soda
1 C. old-fashioned rolled oats

Preheat the oven to 375°F. Melt the butter in a medium saucepan and let cool for 2 minutes. In the same pan, beat in the sugar, egg, and salt until smooth. Stir in the flour and baking soda until almost combined. Stir in the oats until evenly distributed.

Line baking sheets with parchment paper and drop dough by the level half-teaspoon onto the baking sheets, spacing at least 1½" apart. (The dough spreads to make 2" cookies.) Bake the cookies for 7 to 9 minutes, until the centers are golden and fully cooked—the cookies will be well-browned. If underdone, the cookies will not be crisp. Let the cookies cool on the baking sheets for 1 minute, then slide the paper with the cookies onto a wire rack to cool. After about 2 minutes, the cookies will release easily from the parchment.

PEANUT BUTTER FILLING

4 oz. (half of an 8-oz. pkg.) cream
   cheese, at room temperature

½ C. creamy peanut butter
¼ C. packed dark brown sugar

In a small bowl, beat together the cream cheese, peanut butter, and brown sugar until fluffy. Spread approximately 2 teaspoons filling on 1 cookie. Top with another cookie.

CHOCOLATE FILLING

4 oz. semisweet or bittersweet
  chocolate, chopped

1 Tbs. vegetable shortening

In the top of a double boiler set over simmering water, melt the chocolate and shortening together until smooth. Cool until of spreading consistency, about 5 minutes. Spread approximately 2 teaspoons filling on 1 cookie. Top with another cookie.

Crisp Butter Cutouts

These are my favorite butter cookies. Just a bit sweeter than traditional short-bread and topped with large granules of crunchy sugar, they are heaven for butter lovers. The secret to their great flavor is in the baking—let them get well browned on the edges for an intense buttery flavor and crunch. Omit the sugar topping and the dough is perfect for holiday cutouts. Simply frost and decorate them and give as gifts for Valentine's Day, Christmas ornaments, Easter, you name it. I've made puzzle cookies with this dough, too: Roll the dough into a rectangle, chill, and use a sharp knife to cut into jigsaw-like pieces. After the cookie is baked, you can decorate it and let little ones try their hand at putting the puzzle back together.

MAKES 4 DOZEN (2½" TO 3") COOKIES.

1 C. unsalted butter, soft
¾ C. sugar
½ C. powdered sugar
1 large egg
1 tsp. vanilla extract
¾ tsp. salt

3 C. all-purpose flour
½ tsp. baking soda
Washed raw cane sugar, demerara
    sugar, or any large-grained sugar
    for sprinkling (optional)

In a large bowl, beat the butter and sugars until fluffy with no lumps, 1 to 2 minutes. Stir in the egg, vanilla, and salt until the dough is smooth and creamy. Stir in the flour and baking soda until combined. Form the dough into a rough rectangle; wrap in plastic and refrigerate until firm, 30 minutes to 1 hour.

Preheat the oven to 350°F. Divide the dough in half. Between sheets of parchment paper, roll out half the dough into a rectangle ³⁄₁₆" to ¼" thick. Freeze the sheet of rolled dough until firm, 15 minutes. While waiting, roll out the other half of the dough in the same fashion. (You can stack the sheets of rolled dough, separated by parchment, on a sheet pan or cookie sheet in the freezer.) Cut out the cookies, using one chilled sheet of dough at time, and transfer the cookies to parchment-lined baking sheets. Sprinkle with raw sugar, if desired. Bake for 13 to 15 minutes, until the edges are well-browned. Let the cookies cool on the baking sheets for 3 minutes before transferring to wire racks to cool completely.

Double Ginger Butter Crisps

These ultra-crisp, buttery cookies are lighter in texture than traditional gingersnaps. Crystallized ginger not only ups the ginger ante, but the tiny bits also offer an interesting textural contrast to the airy, crisp butter wafer. They are great to serve after dinner.

MAKES 1½ DOZEN (2½") COOKIES.

1 C. all-purpose flour
⅓ C. packed dark brown sugar
1½ tsp. ground ginger
¼ tsp. salt
½ C. unsalted butter, cold

2 Tbs. packed minced crystallized
 ginger
2 Tbs. demerara or raw cane sugar
 for sprinkling (optional)

In a large bowl, combine the flour, sugar, ground ginger, and salt. Cut the butter into ½" chunks and add to the dry ingredients. Using your fingers or a pastry blender, cut in the butter and crystallized ginger until a dough begins to form, but very small chunks of butter are still visible. Form the dough into a rough rectangle; wrap in plastic and refrigerate until firm enough to roll, 15 to 20 minutes.

Preheat the oven to 350°F. Between sheets of parchment paper, roll out the dough into a rectangle approximately 3/16" thick. Freeze the sheet of rolled dough until firm, 15 minutes. Cut out the cookies and transfer to parchment-lined baking sheets. Brush the tops with cold water and sprinkle with the demerara sugar, if desired. Bake for 14 to 16 minutes for 2½" cutouts or until the edges are browned and the centers completely cooked through. Let the cookies cool on the baking sheets for 3 minutes before transferring to wire racks to cool completely.

Lemon–Poppy Seed Cutouts

Rolled thin and crisp, these cookies make a great teatime treat, and are delicious served with lemon curd, sorbet, or berries. A tart, lemony glaze is a nice touch—just take a cup of powdered sugar and stir in fresh lemon juice a teaspoon at a time until the glaze is thin enough to drizzle over the cookies. These are sturdy enough to use for Christmas cookies, too. For the best flavor, lightly toast the poppy seeds in a medium-hot skillet until fragrant, 1 to 2 minutes.

MAKES 3 DOZEN (3") COOKIES.

1 C. unsalted butter, soft	2 large egg yolks
½ C. sugar	1 Tbs. fresh lemon juice
½ C. powdered sugar	½ tsp. salt
2 Tbs. grated lemon zest (from a plane-style grater)	2⅔ C. all-purpose flour
	¼ C. poppy seeds

In a large bowl, beat the butter, sugars, and lemon zest until fluffy with no lumps, 1 to 2 minutes. Stir in the egg yolks, lemon juice, and salt until smooth. Stir in the flour and poppy seeds until combined. Form the dough into a rough rectangle; wrap in plastic and refrigerate until firm, 30 minutes to 1 hour.

Preheat the oven to 350°F. Between sheets of parchment paper, roll out the dough into a rectangle ⅛" to ³⁄₁₆" thick. Freeze the sheet of rolled dough until firm, 15 minutes. Cut out the cookies and transfer to parchment-lined baking sheets. Bake for 12 to 14 minutes for 3" cutouts or until the edges are browned and the cookies are crisp. Let the cookies cool on the baking sheets for 3 minutes before transferring to wire racks to cool completely.

Maple Walnut Leaves

The wafting aroma of maple and toasty walnuts as these cookies bake on a cool, crisp, clear fall day heralds the start of the holiday season, when my nesting instincts kick into high gear and a warm, cozy kitchen is the best space in the house. Leaf- or acorn-shaped cutters are widely available and make beautiful cookies to present on tea trays. Use maple extract if you can find it or the highest-quality maple flavoring you can find to avoid off flavors. Penzeys and King Arthur are both good sources. And don't skimp on the raw sugar; the crunch is addictive.

MAKES 3 DOZEN (2½" TO 3") COOKIES.

½ C. unsalted butter, soft
⅓ C sugar
⅓ C. packed light brown sugar
1 large egg yolk
½ tsp. vanilla extract
¼ tsp. maple flavoring
¼ tsp. salt

1½ C. all-purpose flour
¾ C. finely chopped toasted
   walnuts
Washed raw cane sugar, demerara
   sugar, or any large-grained sugar
   for sprinkling

In a large bowl, beat the butter and sugars until fluffy with no lumps, 1 to 2 minutes. Stir in the egg yolk, vanilla, maple flavoring, and salt until the dough is smooth and creamy. Stir in the flour and walnuts until combined. Form the dough into a rough rectangle; wrap in plastic and refrigerate until firm, 30 minutes to 1 hour.

Preheat the oven to 350°F. Between sheets of parchment paper, roll out the dough into a rectangle ⅛" to ³⁄₁₆" thick. Freeze the sheet of rolled dough until firm, 15 minutes. Cut out the cookies and transfer to parchment-lined baking sheets. Sprinkle with raw sugar. Bake for 11 to 13 minutes for 2½" cutouts or until the bottoms and sides are deep gold and the cookies are crisp. Let the cookies cool on the baking sheets for 3 minutes before transferring to wire racks to cool completely.

Buttery Jam-Filled Linzer Thins

These pretty, delicate, fine-textured cutouts are great for a coffee or tea break. While prepared preserves are fine, these cookies are worthy of home-made jam. I make skillet jam all the time with whatever fruit I have on hand that's just on the verge of being too ripe to last another day. It's fast, easy, has great fresh flavor (unlike longer-cooked preserves), and—best of all—you don't have to drag out the canner and be in front of the stove all day. These cookies are also yummy with hazelnuts in place of the almonds and filled with blackberry jam—my tribute to the bounty here in Oregon. And have fun with decorative cutouts anytime, not just at Christmas. I particularly love flower cutouts: The petals get nice browned edges and the brilliantly colored jam looks gorgeous in the centers.

MAKES 2 DOZEN (2½") SANDWICH COOKIES.

½ C. lightly toasted whole almonds
1 C. unsalted butter, soft
⅓ C. sugar
¼ C. powdered sugar
1 large egg yolk
½ tsp. salt
2 C. plus 2 Tbs. all-purpose flour
½ tsp. ground cinnamon

⅔ C. good-quality prepared
    raspberry jam, thinned with 1 to
    2 Tbs. Chambord, framboise, or
    any berry-friendly liqueur such as
    Cointreau or Grand Marnier, or
    Skillet Jam (see below)
Powdered sugar for dusting

Grind the nuts in a rotary cheese grater; reserve. In a large bowl, beat the butter and sugars until fluffy with no lumps, 1 to 2 minutes. Stir in the egg yolk and salt until the dough is smooth and creamy. Stir in the flour, cinnamon, and reserved nuts until combined. Form the dough into a rough rectangle; wrap in plastic and refrigerate until firm, 30 minutes to 1 hour.

Preheat the oven to 350°F. Divide the dough in half. Between sheets of parchment paper, roll out half of the dough into a rectangle ⅛" to 3⁄16" thick. Freeze the sheet of rolled dough until firm, 15 minutes. While waiting, roll out other half of the dough in the same fashion. (You can stack the sheets of rolled dough, separated by parchment, on a sheet pan or cookie sheet in the freezer.) Cut out the cookies, using one chilled sheet of dough at time, and transfer the cookies to parchment-lined baking sheets. Cut out ½" to ¾" holes in half of the cookies. Bake for 8 to 10 minutes, until the cookies are puffed in the centers and lightly browned on the edges. Let the cookies stand on the baking sheets for 3 minutes before transferring to wire racks to cool.

Spoon about ¾ teaspoon jam into the center of each whole cookie. Dust the remaining cookies (the ones with the holes) liberally with powdered sugar. Top each jam cookie with a powdered sugar cookie.

SKILLET JAM

Easy and versatile! In a medium skillet (or saucepan) over medium heat, combine some berries (raspberries, strawberries, blackberries, Marionberries, blueberries, currants, cranberries, or any combination that appeals to you) or chopped stone fruit (peaches, nectarines, plums, or apricots) that you have on hand with sugar to taste. For fruit that is not extremely ripe or is a bit on the hard side, add 2 to 3 tablespoons of water per cup of fruit so that it can soften as it cooks without burning. Cook until the fruit just begins to fall apart. Dissolve 1 teaspoon cornstarch in 1 tablespoon water per 1 cup of cooked fruit and add to the pan. (Just eyeball it; it'll be fine.) Bring to a boil, stirring constantly. Cook until the mixture just begins to thicken. Refrigerate for up to 2 weeks.

Thumbprint Cookies, Two Ways

As I get older, I've come to love the same sorts of cookies my grandmothers enjoyed, namely anything buttery, nutty, and filled with fresh preserves. As a child, I would not have wasted my time on such boring teatime treats—I was all about chocolate. To please kids and grown-ups alike, I've created a couple of flavor variations of these old-fashioned cookies. Essentially, the dough is a shortbread, but with a touch more sugar, less flour (because of the nuts), and an egg yolk to bind the dough. Jam-filled cookies may be frozen, but not the chocolate-filled ones—freeze the unfilled cookies instead and fill with chocolate after they've thawed. Die-hard chocolate fans can use the Chocolate Shortbread dough on page 113 as the base for these cookies and top with the ganache filling.

MAKES ABOUT 3½ DOZEN COOKIES.

½ C. toasted whole almonds or
   toasted skinned whole hazelnuts
½ C. unsalted butter, soft
¼ C. plus 2 Tbs. sugar
1 large egg yolk
½ tsp. vanilla extract

1 to 2 drops almond extract
   (optional)
¼ tsp. salt
¾ C. plus 2 Tbs. all-purpose flour
½ C. raspberry or Marionberry jam

Grind the nuts in a rotary cheese grater; reserve. In a large bowl, beat the butter and sugar until fluffy with no lumps, 1 to 2 minutes. Stir in the egg yolk, vanilla, almond extract, if desired, and salt until the dough is smooth and creamy. Stir in the flour and ground nuts until combined. Refrigerate the dough until firm enough to shape, 30 to 40 minutes.

Preheat the oven to 350°F. Line baking sheets with parchment paper. Form the chilled dough into 1" balls and place them 2" apart on the baking sheets. Flatten the tops slightly, and make an impression in the center of each with your finger or the end of a wooden spoon. Bake the cookies for 10 minutes. Remove the cookies from the oven. Using a small spoon, fill each cookie with ½ teaspoon jam. Bake for another 5 to 6 minutes, until the edges are lightly browned and crisp. (If you prefer to fill the cookies with chocolate, bake the cookies straight through and fill the cooled cookies.) Let the cookies stand on the baking sheets for 3 minutes before transferring to wire racks to cool.

CHOCOLATE GANACHE FILLING

¼ cup heavy whipping cream

2 oz. semisweet or bittersweet
   chocolate, chopped

1 Tbs. unsalted butter

In a very small saucepan, bring the cream to a boil over medium-high heat. Remove the pan from the heat and add the chocolate. Let stand for 1 minute; stir until completely melted. Stir in the butter until smooth. Let cool until no longer hot, about 5 minutes. Fill the completely cooled cookies with ½ to ¾ teaspoon ganache. The ganache will set up slowly but remain slightly tender. The filled cookies may be stored at room temperature.

Honey Graham Cookies

Though they're made with whole wheat flour, these honey-scented crisps are most definitely cookies, not crackers, as each buttery bite will confirm. They make a great tea cookie served plain, but kids will love to spread peanut butter and jelly on them. You can reduce the butter by ¼ cup and replace it with ½ cup milk for a less-rich treat, but it does change the texture of the cookies (less delicately crisp, a bit harder). If you have little ones, they'll love to make animal cookie cutouts with this dough.

MAKES 2½ TO 3 DOZEN COOKIES.

1 C. unsalted butter	¼ tsp. ground cinnamon
½ C. packed light brown sugar	1½ C. all-purpose flour
¼ C. honey	1 C. whole wheat flour
¾ tsp. salt	

Melt half of the butter in a medium saucepan. Remove the pan from the heat and let stand for 1 minute. Cut the remaining butter into pieces and add to the pan; let stand for 1 minute. Add the brown sugar, honey, and salt to the pan, stirring to combine. Stir in the cinnamon and the flours. Form the dough into a rough rectangle; wrap in plastic and refrigerate until firm, 30 minutes to 1 hour.

Preheat the oven to 350°F. Between sheets of parchment paper, roll out the dough into a rectangle ⅛" to 3/16" thick. Freeze the sheet of rolled dough until firm, 15 minutes. Cut out the cookies and place on parchment-lined baking sheets. For 2½" cutouts, bake for 15 to 18 minutes, until the edges and tops are browned. If you choose to make the milk version, they will require a second baking to make them crisp: Reduce the oven temperature to 275°F. Transfer the baked cookies to a wire rack set over a sheet pan and return to the oven to bake for another 10 minutes or until crisp. Let the cookies stand on the baking sheets for 3 minutes before transferring to wire racks to cool.

Espresso Gingerbread Cutouts

This gingerbread dough makes beautiful cutouts that retain their shape—a difficult accomplishment for a cookie with a lot of butter and molasses. I love the addition of espresso powder, which adds a smoky flavor note to the spicy cookies. I make the dough ahead and refrigerate it for at least 24 hours to let the flavors meld. Royal icing is the traditional way to decorate fancy cut-out cookies at Christmastime, but at other times of the year, I cut out plain circles and top the baked cookies with a powdered sugar–espresso glaze or simply drizzle the cookies with melted chocolate. (For glaze, stir brewed espresso or reconstituted espresso powder a teaspoon at a time into a cup of powdered sugar until smooth and thin enough to drizzle.)

MAKES 4 DOZEN (2½" TO 3") COOKIES.

1 C. unsalted butter, soft	¾ tsp. salt
¾ C. sugar	3¼ C. all-purpose flour
¾ C. packed brown sugar	1 tsp. baking soda
2 Tbs. dark molasses, preferably Barbados style	2 tsp. ground ginger
	1 tsp. ground cinnamon
1 large egg	¼ tsp. freshly grated nutmeg
2 Tbs. instant espresso powder	⅛ tsp. ground cloves

In a large bowl, beat the butter, sugars, and molasses until fluffy with no lumps, 1 to 2 minutes. Stir in the egg, espresso powder, and salt until the dough is smooth and creamy. Stir in the flour, baking soda, and spices, until combined. Form the dough into a rough rectangle; wrap in plastic and refrigerate for 24 hours.

Preheat the oven to 350°F. Divide the dough in half. Between sheets of parchment paper, roll out half of the dough into a rectangle ³⁄₁₆" to ¼" thick. Freeze the sheet of rolled dough until firm, 15 minutes. While waiting, roll out the other half of the dough in the same fashion. (You can stack the sheets of rolled dough, separated by parchment, on a sheet pan or cookie sheet in the freezer.) Cut out the cookies, using one chilled sheet of dough at time, and transfer the cookies to parchment-lined baking sheets. Bake for 12 to 15 minutes, until the edges are firm and the centers are set. Let the cookies cool on the baking sheets for 3 minutes before transferring to wire racks to cool completely.

Chocolate Shortbread

I am always amazed at the flavor of these cookies—the first bite yields a hit of intense, dark chocolate flavor, but the finish is pure, buttery goodness. The trickiest part of making perfect chocolate shortbread is getting the baking just right. Because the dough is already dark, you can't discern browning easily. Remember browning is a chemical reaction that creates wonderful flavor, not just a visual change. Perfectly cooked shortbread is crisp and supremely buttery—not pasty or mealy. Because cooled shortbread is brittle, it's best to score the cookies with the tip of a sharp knife or even a serrated knife when just out of the oven. Then, cut through the scored lines when the bars are just barely warm to the touch. They will keep for nearly a week in an airtight container.

MAKES 2 DOZEN SMALL COOKIES.

½ C. unsalted butter, almost meltingly soft   ¼ tsp. salt
6 Tbs. packed light brown sugar   ¼ C. unsweetened cocoa powder
½ tsp. vanilla extract   ¾ C. all-purpose flour

In a large bowl, beat the butter, sugar, vanilla, and salt until fluffy with no lumps, about 1 minute. Stir in the cocoa and then the flour until well combined.

Roll the dough into a ¼"-thick rough rectangle between sheets of parchment paper. Prick the dough all over with a fork and refrigerate for 30 minutes. Transfer the dough sheet with its bottom layer of parchment paper to a baking sheet.

Preheat the oven to 325°F. Bake for 25 minutes, until firm in the center and the edges are browned (more brown than rest of the dough—this will be hard to tell). Using a very sharp or serrated knife, score the dough into 1" by 1½" pieces. Cool for 5 to 10 minutes. Cut into pieces along the scored lines. Transfer the cookies to a wire rack set over a baking sheet; bake for 5 minutes or until crisp.

→ **ALTERNATIVE METHOD:** Press the dough into a foil-lined 8"-square baking pan. Prick all over with a fork and chill for 30 minutes. Bake as directed for the first baking of the rolled dough and score while still warm, but cool completely before removing from the pan so the cookies do not crack or crumble. After you remove the dough from the pan, cut into pieces. Cookies baked in a rectangular pan are easiest to remove if the paper or foil hangs over the edge of the pan to use as handles to lift out the baked cookie block.

Coconut-Almond Lace Tuiles

These fancy cookies are great to have in your repertoire—they can be formed into very elegant cornucopias holding liqueur-flavored whipped cream or into festive little dessert cups that can hold sorbet, ice cream, or mousse. And don't just make them for special occasions—lacy, delicate, and full of caramel crunchiness, the cookies are wonderful plain, served with an after-dinner sip of Cognac. If you want to dress them up, simply drizzle with a bit of melted chocolate. Feel free to substitute your favorite nuts in place of the almonds—pecans and hazelnuts are also lovely.

MAKES 12 TUILES.

¼ C. unsalted butter
⅓ C. packed light brown sugar
2 Tbs. corn syrup
¼ C. all-purpose flour
¼ tsp. salt

½ C. loosely packed sweetened
   flaked coconut
3 Tbs. very finely chopped toasted
   almonds

Preheat the oven to 375°F. In a medium saucepan, bring the butter, brown sugar, and corn syrup to a boil over medium-high heat, stirring. Add the flour and salt; cook, stirring constantly until the dough thickens, about 1 minute. Stir in the coconut and the almonds and let cool for 5 minutes.

Butter an 18" x 12" baking sheet and drop the dough by scant tablespoons onto the baking sheet, staggering them, only 6 cookies at a time. (The dough spreads to make 4½" cookies.) Pat each dough mound into a 2" round with your fingertips. Bake the cookies for 6 to 8 minutes, until golden all over and deep brown on the edges. (Underbaked cookies will be chewy rather than crisp after they cool.) Bake and form just one baking sheet of cookies at time in order have the maximum window of time for shaping successfully.

Let the cookies cool on the baking sheet until just firm enough to handle, about 2 minutes. Gently loosen the cookies with an offset spatula. The still-warm cookies can be rolled into cone shapes around buttered aluminum foil molds or draped over the bottoms of buttered juice glasses to form dessert cups for mousse or ice cream. If the cookies do become too brittle to form, return the baking sheet with the cookies to the oven for a few seconds to soften. The cookies are also excellent flat.

Almond & Hazelnut Crunch Biscotti

Perfect biscotti have a deep, burnished toffee-butterscotch flavor and are perfectly crisp. They should shatter, not crumble into mealy bits, when you bite into them. Oil, most true to Italian recipes, rather than butter, is the secret to this texture. Filled with heart-healthy fats from the nuts, these cookies are high in protein and are a great afternoon pick-me-up. Blanched almonds, which have their skins removed, make the prettiest cookies, but don't worry if natural almonds are what you have on hand. I love the flavor of hazelnuts, but since their flavor is assertive and easily overpowers the flavor of almonds, I use much less of them. Hazelnuts almost always have their skins on when you buy them—after toasting them in the oven, simply rub skins from cooled hazelnuts. You'll notice this recipe calls for what appears to be a crazy amount of almond extract—don't worry, this is not excessive for a cookie packed with nuts. I love to grind the nuts in a rotary cheese grater—it beats the food processor any day. The nuts never get heavy or oily, but stay light and powdery, which makes for a lighter-textured cookie. Biscotti get better with time—they'll keep for nearly a month, and indeed, their flavor intensifies a few days after baking.

MAKES ABOUT 6 DOZEN COOKIES.

1½ C. lightly toasted whole almonds (divided)	2½ tsp. baking powder
½ C. lightly toasted whole hazelnuts, skinned	½ tsp. salt
	¼ tsp. ground cinnamon
2 C. all-purpose flour	3 large eggs
⅔ C. sugar	3 Tbs. oil
⅔ C. packed brown sugar	2 tsp. almond extract
	2 tsp. vanilla extract

Preheat the oven to 325°F. Coarsely chop 1 cup of the almonds and all of the hazelnuts; reserve. Grind the remaining ½ cup almonds in a rotary cheese grater. In a large bowl, combine the ground nuts with the flour, sugars, baking powder, salt, and cinnamon. If the brown sugar is lumpy, sift it through a wire mesh strainer. Stir in the reserved chopped nuts.

In a liquid measuring cup, beat the eggs, oil, and extracts together until smooth. Stir just enough of the egg mixture into the dry ingredients to form a rather dry, shaggy dough. If too much liquid is added, the dough will become sticky, loose, and difficult to shape. Reserve the remaining egg mixture. Knead the dough briefly to smooth it out and incorporate all remaining dry particles.

Divide the dough into two pieces. Wet your hands with water to prevent sticking and roll each piece of dough into a log about 12" long, flattening the top until the log is 1½" high. Line a large (18" x 12") baking sheet with parchment paper and place the logs on the baking sheet, spacing them at least 5" apart. Brush the tops with the reserved egg mixture.

Bake for 25 to 30 minutes, until the edges of the logs are browned and firm and the centers of the logs have puffed and developed a skin, but are still slightly soft. Let the cookie logs cool for 30 minutes to 1 hour, then gently slice them crosswise with a large serrated knife into ½"-thick slices. Lower the oven temperature to 300°F, return the sliced biscotti to the baking sheet, bottom-side down, and bake for another 20 to 30 minutes, until golden, crisp, and dry.

Chocolate Biscotti

Because I am American, I had to make a deep, dark, and truly chocolaty version of Italian biscotti. Forget espresso—an ice cold glass of milk will be necessary after one of these cookies. Still, they're much lower in fat than typical cookies, so if you end up eating two or three, no worries. Crunchy Chocolate Biscotti are the perfect accompaniment to a bowl of ice cream. The biscotti owe their rich, fudgy flavor to the addition of mini chocolate chips. Unfortunately the added chocolate also makes them irresistible.

MAKES ABOUT 6 DOZEN COOKIES.

1½ C. lightly toasted whole almonds (divided)
1½ C. all-purpose flour
1½ C. sugar (divided)
⅔ C. unsweetened cocoa powder
2½ tsp. baking powder

½ tsp. salt
1 C. mini semisweet chocolate chips
4 large eggs
3 Tbs. oil
2 tsp. almond extract
2 tsp. vanilla extract

Preheat the oven to 325°F. Coarsely chop 1 cup of the almonds; reserve. Grind the remaining almonds in a rotary cheese grater. In a large bowl, combine the ground nuts with the flour, 1¼ cup plus 2 tablespoons of the sugar, the cocoa powder, baking powder, and salt. Stir in the chocolate chips and the reserved chopped nuts.

In a liquid measuring cup, beat the eggs, oil, and extracts together until smooth. Stir just enough of the egg mixture into the dry ingredients to form a rather dry, shaggy dough. If too much liquid is added, the dough will become sticky, loose, and difficult to shape. Reserve the remaining egg mixture. Knead the dough briefly to smooth it out and incorporate all remaining dry particles.

Divide the dough into two pieces. Wet your hands with water to prevent sticking and roll each piece of dough into a log about 12" long, flattening the top until the log is 1½" high. Line a large (18" x 12") baking sheet with parchment paper and place the logs on the baking sheet, spacing them at least 5" apart. Brush the tops with the reserved egg mixture, and sprinkle with the remaining 2 Tbs. sugar.

Bake for 25 to 30 minutes, until the edges of the logs are browned and firm and the centers of the logs have puffed and developed a skin, but are still slightly soft. Let the cookie logs cool for 30 minutes to 1 hour, then gently slice them crosswise with a large serrated knife into ½"-thick slices. Lower the oven temperature to 300°F, return the sliced biscotti to the baking sheet, bottom-side down, and bake for another 20 to 30 minutes, until crisp and dry.

Pistachio Biscotti with Dried Cherries

I love the tart zippiness that the fresh lemon zest and cherries or cranberries add to this recipe. But, if you have to satisfy a chocolate craving, omit the lemon, reduce the dried fruit to a half cup, and add a half cup of mini chocolate chips for a very nice Neapolitan-inspired cookie.

MAKES ABOUT 6 DOZEN COOKIES.

1½ C. lightly toasted shelled pistachios (divided)
2 C. all-purpose flour
1¼ C. sugar
1 Tbs. grated lemon zest
2½ tsp. baking powder

½ tsp. salt
1 C. dried tart cherries or cranberries
3 large eggs
3 Tbs. oil
½ tsp. almond extract
1 tsp. vanilla extract

Preheat the oven to 325°F. Coarsely chop 1 cup of the pistachios; reserve. Grind the remaining pistachios in a rotary cheese grater. In a large bowl, combine the ground nuts with the flour, sugar, lemon zest, baking powder, and salt. Stir in the dried fruit and the reserved chopped nuts.

In a liquid measuring cup, beat the eggs, oil, and extracts together until smooth. Stir just enough of the egg mixture into the dry ingredients to form a rather dry, shaggy dough. If too much liquid is added, the dough will become sticky, loose, and difficult to shape. Reserve the remaining egg mixture. Knead the dough briefly to smooth it out and incorporate all remaining dry particles.

Divide the dough into two pieces. Wet your hands with water to prevent sticking and roll each piece of dough into a log about 12" long, flattening the top until the log is 1½" high. Line a large (18" x 12") baking sheet with parchment paper and place the logs on the baking sheet, spacing them at least 5" apart. Brush the tops with the reserved egg mixture.

Bake for 25 to 30 minutes, until the edges of the logs are browned and firm and the centers of the logs have puffed and developed a skin, but are still slightly soft. Let the cookie logs cool for 30 minutes to 1 hour, then gently slice them crosswise with a large serrated knife into ½"-thick slices. Lower the oven temperature to 300°F, return the sliced biscotti to the baking sheet, bottom-side down, and bake for another 20 to 30 minutes, until golden, crisp, and dry.

This is one of my very favorite cookies—the bright, tart flavor of the cranberries accentuates the intensely buttery flavor of the shortbread crust and topping. The recipe appeared in *Fine Cooking*, when I did a shortbread bar cookie story for the magazine. The story proved to be an opportunity to tinker with the best method of coaxing the most butter flavor out of a simple shortbread recipe—perhaps I don't need to say this at this point in the book, but I'm crazy about the flavor of butter. Traditional English and Scottish recipes use the creaming method, which makes for tender, light, and airy cookies. Melting the butter first, however, makes for a crunchier cookie that, oddly enough, has a more prominent buttery flavor. Go figure. You can use your favorite prepared preserves or jam to fill these bars, but choose one that is tart rather than sweet for the best flavor combination. Making the cranberry filling takes only 15 minutes (and any ripe fruit you have on hand will work, from withering apricots to sunken blackberries), and the intense, fresh flavor is worth it. Walnut shortbread filled with blackberry jam and almond shortbread filled with sour cherry preserves are my two favorite flavor variations—just add a half cup of finely chopped toasted nuts to the dough for these variations and maybe a touch of almond extract for the almond bars.

MAKES ABOUT 35 SMALL BARS.

CRANBERRY FILLING

1 (12-oz.) bag frozen cranberries, thawed slightly	1 C. sugar
	¼ C. water

Bring all the ingredients to a boil in a saucepan over high heat. Reduce the temperature to medium-high and boil for 5 to 7 minutes, until most of the liquid is evaporated and what is left forms a thick glaze on a spoon. The cranberries should appear to be floating in syrup, not juices, and will thicken further when cooled. Remove the pan from the heat and let the mixture cool for 5 to 10 minutes.

CRUST AND STREUSEL

1⅓ C. unsalted butter, melted and cooled to just warm

1 C. sugar (divided)

2 large egg yolks

¾ tsp. salt

3 C. all-purpose flour

Line a 13" x 9" baking pan with foil, letting the ends create an overhanging edge for easy removal. In a large bowl, stir together the melted butter and ¾ cup of the sugar until just combined. Stir in the egg yolks and salt until smooth. Stir in the flour to make a stiff dough. Transfer about 2 cups of the dough (not the entire amount!) to the prepared pan. Press the mixture evenly into the bottom of the pan. Prick the dough all over with a fork. Refrigerate for 30 minutes (or freeze for 5 to 7 minutes), until the dough is firm.

Meanwhile, for the streusel, with your fingers, combine the remaining ¼ cup sugar with the reserved dough until crumbly. The mixture should hold together when pressed, but readily break into small crumbs. Set aside.

Preheat the oven to 325°F. Bake the crust for 20 minutes, until it begins to set but is not brown at all on the edges (the center will not be firm yet). Take out the crust and increase the oven temperature to 350°F. Spread the cranberry filling evenly over the hot crust. Crumble the streusel over the cranberries. Bake the bars near the top of the oven for 25 minutes, until the streusel is golden and set. (Baking these bars at the top of the oven helps the streusel to brown faster without overbrowning the crust.) Place the pan on a wire rack to cool for 1 to 2 hours. You can speed the process by cooling the bars outside in winter or in the refrigerator once the pan is no longer piping hot. When the bottom of the pan is cool, carefully lift the bars from the pan using the foil overhang and transfer them to a cutting board. Slip the foil away from the bars by lifting with a metal spatula. Cut the bars into 1¾" squares.

Lemon Squares

These lemon squares are tart, with a buttery shortbread base that's not too sweet. I add toasted hazelnuts to the crust, but lemon purists may omit them. If you love lemon meringue pie, you can top the bars with meringue (see page 203).

(see page 203).

MAKES 2 DOZEN BARS.

SHORTBREAD CRUST

14 Tbs. unsalted butter, melted and cooled to just warm

½ C. sugar

½ tsp. salt

2 C. all-purpose flour

¼ C. toasted hazelnuts or almonds, skinned (optional)

Line a 13" x 9" baking pan with foil, leaving an overhanging edge for easy removal. Lightly butter the sides of foil (not the bottom) to prevent the lemon curd from sticking. In a medium bowl, stir together the butter, sugar, and salt until just combined. Add the flour and then, using a rotary grater, grate the hazelnuts directly on top of the flour. Stir until dough just comes together. Press the mixture evenly into the pan. Prick the dough with a fork. Refrigerate for 30 minutes (or freeze for 5 to 7 minutes), until the dough is firm.

Preheat the oven to 325°F. Bake for 25 minutes, until the crust begins to set but has not begun to brown at the edges (the center will not be firm yet).

LEMON CURD

4 large eggs

1¼ C. sugar

3 Tbs. all-purpose flour

⅛ tsp. salt

¾ C. fresh lemon juice

1 Tbs. grated lemon zest (from a plane-style grater)

Powdered sugar for dusting

In a medium bowl, whisk together the eggs, sugar, flour, and salt until smooth, about 1 minute. Whisk in the lemon juice and zest. Pour the filling over the hot crust. Return the pan to oven and increase the heat to 350°F. Bake for 20 minutes or until the center is set and the edges are golden. The topping will no longer wiggle when the pan is moved. Place the pan on a wire rack to cool for 1 to 2 hours. When the bottom of the pan is cool, carefully lift the bars from the pan using the foil overhang and transfer them to a cutting board. Dust with powdered sugar before serving. Cut into 2" squares.

Fig Bars

These fig bars are substantial in heft and sophisticated in flavor—perfect for grown-ups. You can serve them with a glass of milk or a sip of bourbon. I've made fig bars with the traditional sweet pastry dough, but I prefer the crunch and richness of streusel, which is never soggy or dry. The filling is based on Italian recipes for fig cookies, which often feature orange, spices, and rum. If you are feeling decadent, fold chopped bittersweet chocolate into the cooled fig filling, or drizzle the top of the bars with chocolate ganache and toasted sliced almonds. You can mix different dried fruits together for the filling and use red wine or even crushed pineapple for the cooking liquid instead of orange juice.

MAKES 2 DOZEN BARS.

FIG FILLING

2 C. dried Mission figs,
  finely chopped
1 C. fresh orange juice
½ tsp. grated orange zest

¼ C. honey
¼ C. packed light brown sugar
½ tsp. ground cinnamon
2 Tbs. dark rum, Cognac, or whiskey

Combine all the ingredients in a medium saucepan over high heat with enough water to cover. Bring to a boil; reduce the heat to medium-low. Simmer the mixture, covered, until tender, adding more water if necessary. Moist figs will become tender in about 10 minutes, while drier figs may take up to 30 minutes and a fair amount more water. After the figs are soft, using a wooden spoon or a potato masher if necessary, mash into a rough puree. Use immediately or refrigerate for up to 2 weeks. If you do make the mixture ahead of time, when you're ready to use it you may have to add a few tablespoons of lukewarm water to make the mixture spreadable.

CRUST AND STREUSEL

1⅓ C. unsalted butter, melted and
  cooled to just warm
1 C. packed light brown sugar
  (divided)

2 large egg yolks
¾ tsp. salt
3 C. all-purpose flour

Line a 13" x 9" baking pan with foil, letting the ends create an overhanging edge for easy removal. In a large bowl, stir together the melted butter and ¾ cup of the brown sugar until just combined. Stir in the egg yolks and salt until smooth. Stir in the flour to make a stiff dough. Transfer about 2 cups of the dough (not the entire amount!) to the prepared pan. Press the mixture evenly into the bottom of the pan. Prick the dough all over with a fork. Refrigerate for 30 minutes (or freeze for 5 to 7 minutes), until the dough is firm.

Meanwhile, for the streusel, with your fingers, combine the remaining ¼ cup brown sugar with the reserved dough until crumbly. The mixture should hold together when pressed, but readily break into small crumbs. Set aside.

Preheat the oven to 325°F. Bake the crust for 20 minutes, until the crust begins to set but is not brown at all on the edges (the center will not be firm yet). Take out the crust and increase the oven temperature to 350°F. Spread the fig filling evenly over the hot crust. Crumble the streusel over the fig filling. Bake the bars near the top of the oven for 20 to 25 minutes, until the streusel is golden and set. (Baking these bars at the top of the oven helps the streusel to brown faster without overbrowning the crust.) Place the pan on a wire rack to cool for 1 to 2 hours. You can speed the process by cooling the bars outside in winter or in the refrigerator once the pan is no longer piping hot. When the bottom of the pan is cool, carefully lift the bars from the pan using the foil overhang and transfer them to a cutting board. Slip the foil away from the bars by lifting with a metal spatula. Cut into 2" squares.

Caramel Turtle Bars

Most of us have fond childhood memories of some sort of turtle candy cluster . . . that irresistible combination of caramel, pecans, and chocolate that marked hands and face with telltale signs. The rich shortbread cookie crust on these bars not only provides a slightly cleaner delivery mechanism, but it also stands up well under a mother lode of pecans, caramel, and bittersweet ganache that'd make a pastry crust soggy after a day or two. The "caramel" here is stress free and foolproof—not actually a true caramel, achieved at around 310°F, but a simple cooked buttery brown sugar filling that delivers caramel flavor without the angst of having to stare at a candy thermometer. This recipe is also very tasty with walnuts, almonds, or even macadamia nuts.

MAKES 4 DOZEN BARS.

SHORTBREAD CRUST

14 Tbs. unsalted butter, melted and cooled to just warm
½ C. packed light brown sugar
½ tsp. salt
2 C. all-purpose flour

Line a 13" x 9" baking pan with foil, leaving an overhanging edge for easy removal. Lightly butter the sides of foil (not the bottom) to prevent the caramel from sticking. In a medium bowl, stir together the butter, sugar, and salt until just combined. Stir in the flour to make a stiff dough. Press the mixture evenly into the bottom of the pan. Prick the dough with a fork. Refrigerate for 30 minutes (or freeze for 5 to 7 minutes), until the dough is firm.

Preheat the oven to 325°F. Bake for 20 minutes, then lower the oven temperature to 300°F and bake for 15 more minutes, until the crust is golden all over and completely set. Set aside on a wire rack.

TURTLE TOPPING

1 C. packed light brown sugar
¾ C. plus 6 Tbs. heavy whipping cream (divided)
½ C. unsalted butter, cut into chunks
½ C. light corn syrup
¼ tsp. salt
2 C. pecan halves, toasted and coarsely chopped
2 oz. bittersweet chocolate, chopped

In a medium heavy saucepan over medium-high heat, bring the brown sugar, ¾ cup of the heavy cream, the butter, corn syrup, and salt to a boil, stirring until smooth. Continue boiling, without stirring, for 6 minutes. Meanwhile, sprinkle the pecans over the baked shortbread crust. Pour the hot caramel evenly over the pecans. Let cool completely at room temperature, about 2 hours.

In a small saucepan over high heat, bring the remaining heavy cream to a boil. Remove from the heat; add the chopped chocolate and stir until smooth and melted. Drizzle the chocolate mixture with a fork over the cooled bars. Let the chocolate set up for 30 minutes to 1 hour. Carefully lift the bars from the pan using the foil overhang and transfer them to a cutting board. Slip the foil away from the bars by lifting with a metal spatula. Cut into 1½" squares and serve at room temperature.

Coffee-Toffee Dream Bars

This is my take on the classic dream bar, or 7-layer bars as they are sometimes called—actually, it's more candy bar than cookie, to be honest. If you grew up in a house where cookies were baked at all, you've probably had some version of it. Not only are these bars real crowd-pleasers, they have the bonus feature of being incredibly fast and easy to make. The chocolate cookie crust and the espresso powder I've added to the condensed milk add a hint of darkness that balances the bars' sweetness. However, for those with a kid's sweet tooth, try a graham cracker crust, pecans, coconut, and chopped white chocolate—it's kind of a cookie version of German chocolate cake frosting.

MAKES ABOUT 42 BARS.

6 Tbs. unsalted butter, melted
1½ C. finely crushed chocolate wafer cookies (about three-quarters of a box of Nabisco Famous Chocolate Wafers)
1 C. toasted coarsely chopped pecans
1 C. loosely packed sweetened flaked coconut

¾ C. toffee baking pieces
¾ C. mini semisweet chocolate chips
1½ Tbs. instant espresso powder
1 (14-oz.) can sweetened condensed milk

Preheat the oven to 350°F. Line a 9"-square baking pan with foil, letting the ends create an overhanging edge for easy removal. Lightly butter the sides of the pan. Pour the melted butter into the pan and then sprinkle evenly with the cookie crumbs. Pat lightly. Sprinkle the toasted pecans, coconut, toffee pieces, and chocolate chips over the crust in layers, one after the other. Stir the espresso powder into the condensed milk until dissolved and then pour over the layered ingredients, covering as evenly as possible.

Bake for 25 to 28 minutes, until golden on the top and bubbly on the edges. Place the pan on a wire rack to cool completely, about 1 hour. When the bottom of the pan is cool, carefully lift the bars from the pan using the foil overhang and transfer them to a cutting board. Slip the foil away from the bars by lifting with a metal spatula. Cut into 2" x 1½" rectangles.

Chewy Trail Bars with Mixed Fruit & Seeds

A recipe by Tish Boyle, author of *The Good Cookie*, inspired these bars. She's the editor of *Chocolatier* magazine, so you know she's got impeccable taste. I make these dense, chewy bars before day trips—packed with nutrition, they make great energy bars. The flavor of honey permeates the bars and keeps them moist for days. For hundreds of years, honey has been used to sweeten "keeping" cakes and bars. Honey, like molasses and corn syrup, attracts moisture from the environment and holds on to it, keeping baked goods moist and soft. Choose a good-quality honey with a flavor you like—I love the deep gold, intriguing flavor of honeys such as chestnut, pine, and buckwheat. I tend to select fruit and nuts that pair well with one another as well as with the honey—almonds and dried apricots, walnuts and dates, pecans and dried cranberries.

MAKES 2 DOZEN BARS.

⅓ C. oil	¾ C. packed light brown sugar
⅓ C. honey	½ tsp. ground cinnamon
1 large egg	½ tsp. ground ginger
1 tsp. vanilla extract	½ tsp. salt
¼ tsp. almond extract	1¼ C. chopped dried fruit
1¾ C. quick-cooking oats	¾ C. chopped toasted nuts
¾ C. all-purpose flour	¼ C. lightly toasted sesame seeds

Preheat the oven to 350°F. Line a 13" x 9" baking pan with foil, leaving an overhanging edge for easy removal. Lightly butter the sides of foil and the bottom to prevent the bars from sticking. In a large bowl, whisk together the oil, honey, egg, and extracts until well combined. Stir in the dry ingredients until combined. The dough will be stiff. Press the mixture evenly into the pan. Bake for 25 minutes or until the middle is set and the edges are golden. Cool for 10 minutes in the pan. Invert the pan onto a cutting board. Remove the pan and peel away the foil. Invert the bars back onto a wire rack to cool completely, about 1 hour. Cut into 2" squares with a buttered knife.

Chocolate has become an object of connoisseurship in the past twenty years—bar chocolate, that is. Cocoa powder, however, has been neglected by foodies during the fervor for premium bars of bittersweet chocolate. This is strange, because unsweetened cocoa is a pure, unadulterated hit of chocolate flavor—something any baker should appreciate. These brownies use cocoa and are surprisingly dark, rich, and moist. The secret is the combination of butter, a fat that is soft at room temperature, and unsweetened cocoa powder. Bar chocolate is hard at room temperature, so it produces brownies that are firm, dense, and candy-like in texture—literally like fudge. You probably have a brownie recipe in your repertoire made with bar chocolate, but you must add this super-moist recipe to your collection. Though these brownies need no adornment, I've included a recipe for ganache frosting for those seeking an over-the-top chocolate experience.

MAKES 16 BROWNIES.

1 C. plus 1 tsp. unsalted butter
2 C. sugar
4 large eggs, at room temperature
½ tsp. vanilla extract
½ tsp. salt

¾ C. unsweetened natural cocoa powder
⅔ C. all-purpose flour
Simple Ganache Frosting (optional; see facing page)

Preheat the oven to 350°F. Butter and flour a 9"-square baking pan. Melt the butter in a medium saucepan. Remove the pan from the heat. Beat in the sugar until well combined, about 1 minute. Beat in the eggs, vanilla, and salt until smooth, about 1 minute. Beat in the cocoa powder and then the flour until smooth and uniform, about 30 seconds.

Spread the batter evenly in the prepared pan. Bake for 35 to 40 minutes, until a wooden skewer inserted ⅔ toward the center comes out with only moist crumbs clinging to it. Let the brownies cool in the pan to just warm before serving plain; otherwise cool completely before frosting with ganache. Cut in 2¼" squares.

SIMPLE GANACHE FROSTING

Ganache is usually a silky combination of cream and chocolate, but many versions abound. Plain chocolate ganache is wonderful, but you can add a hint of other flavors to this ganache by adding a different liquid in place of some of the cream, such as espresso, concentrated tea or chai, liqueur, or even port or wine that has been boiled down in a saucepan to concentrate its flavor.

MAKES GANACHE FOR 16 (2¼") BROWNIES.

¾ C. heavy cream

5 oz. bittersweet chocolate, finely chopped

Bring the heavy cream to a boil in a medium saucepan over medium-high heat, stirring occasionally. Remove the pan from the heat. Add the chopped chocolate (and flavoring of choice, if desired) and stir until the mixture is smooth and melted.

Transfer to a bowl and cover the surface directly with plastic wrap to prevent it from forming a skin. Place in a cool part of the kitchen and let cool to room temperature, stirring occasionally.

Once it feels thick enough to spread, evenly frost the completely cooled brownies with the ganache. Let set up for 30 minutes at room temperature. Cut in 1½" squares and serve at room temperature.

NOTE: Ganache-covered brownies should be kept in the refrigerator if they will not be consumed within 48 hours.

I like to take plain old brownies and dress them up for company. Suddenly they become fanciful little bites that look elegant enough to serve as petits fours. I make the mint-filled brownies during the winter holidays; they're the perfect end to a buffet dinner. Try serving them on the cool side, which enhances the contrast between the refreshing peppermint filling and the rich, dark chocolate.

MAKES 25 BROWNIES.

3 Tbs. unsalted butter, soft
1¾ C. powdered sugar
2 tsp. pure peppermint extract
¾ cup heavy whipping cream
    (divided)

1 baked recipe Moist & Chewy
    Brownies (page 130)
1 (3.5-oz.) bittersweet chocolate bar,
    chopped

In a medium bowl, stir together the butter, sugar, peppermint extract, and 1 to 2 tablespoons of the cream until the mixture is smooth and spreadable. Spread over the baked, cooled brownies. Freeze for 15 minutes. Meanwhile, in a small saucepan, bring the remaining heavy cream to a boil. Remove from the heat and whisk in the chocolate until smooth and melted. Cool slightly, stirring occasionally, for 2 to 3 minutes. Set the cold mint-topped brownies on a wire rack set over a baking pan. Pour the liquid ganache over the brownies and use an offset spatula to spread evenly across the top. Refrigerate until the ganache is set, about 1 hour. Cut into squares and serve cool. (Heat the knife blade under very hot running water and clean the blade with a paper towel between slices for the nicest appearance.)

PB & C Brownies

Brownies are so simple and wonderful that they're the prefect foil for creating new desserts. Even just chopping up your favorite candy bars and adding them to the batter (Mounds candy bars and toasted almonds, or Heath toffee bars and espresso chips) turns something basic into something new. Here, I've recreated my favorite candy bar, Reese's Peanut Butter Cups, as a layered brownie. But you don't need anything more than a basic brownie recipe to have fun in the kitchen. I like to sprinkle marshmallows, chopped chocolate, and nuts over the top of baked brownies and broil for 30 seconds—Voila, Rocky Road Brownies! Let your imagination run wild.

MAKES 25 BROWNIES.

1 C. creamy peanut butter
6 Tbs. unsalted butter, soft
1½ C. powdered sugar (divided)
1 tsp. vanilla extract
1 to 2 Tbs. hot water

1 baked recipe Moist & Chewy
  Brownies (page 130)
1 recipe Simple Ganache Frosting
  (page 131)

In a medium bowl, beat together the peanut butter, butter, sugar, vanilla, and enough of the water to make a smooth and spreadable mixture. Spread the peanut butter mixture over the baked, cooled brownies. Spread the ganache evenly over the peanut butter layer. Let stand at room temperature until set, about 1 hour. Cut into squares and serve at room temperature.

06

CAKES

making cakes is rewarding—the flavor of a home-baked cake is like nothing else. If you grew up with cakes made from mixes, you'll be pleasantly surprised by how easy it is to make one from scratch. Truly, it's no more time-consuming than a cake mix. Why not fill the house with the aroma of real butter, pure vanilla extract, and fine chocolate?

the lazy cook's guide to baking great cakes

you'll notice that each recipe starts out by asking you to preheat the oven and prepare a baking pan. It's better to get these items out of the way so you don't have to stop and wait after the cake batter is mixed—stirring or transferring the batter after it's been sitting for a few minutes can cause it to lose volume, affecting your finished cake. To prepare baking pans, lightly coat the inside with soft or melted butter (use a pastry brush for this), and then dust the pan with flour, tapping out the excess. This will ensure that the finished cake can be removed from the pan without sticking. Old-fashioned recipes call this "greasing the pan," but I think "buttering the pan" sounds more appetizing. The word *grease* is all-purpose, indicating that most people use the same fat that the recipe calls for to coat the pan. I am more particular. I always butter the pan, even if the cake uses oil. Why? Because when the outside edge of a piece of cake hits your tongue, that little bit of butter tastes best.

The secret to great texture in cakes starts with having your ingredients at room temperature. There's a fudge factor with cookies that you don't have in cake baking—you can get away with stirring a cold egg into cookie dough. For cakes, the warm side of room temperature is best. Back in the 1940s and '50s, baking scientists illustrated that a warm cake batter, meaning one between 70°F and 76°F, rose to a greater volume than the same recipe made with a batter 10 degrees cooler.

How a cake batter is mixed also affects the volume and crumb structure of the finished cake. For batters that will be mixed by hand, the *creaming method* creates the best cake structure. With this method, the butter and sugar are beaten together first to incorporate air, and then the eggs are gradually beaten into the butter mixture. This air is important—the baking powder in the recipe will help those tiny air bubbles to expand and make the cake rise in the heat of the oven. When a recipe uses oil instead of butter, beat the eggs and sugar together first to incorporate air, or whip the oil, sugar, and eggs together until creamy and thick.

The flour and remaining dry ingredients, such as baking powder, are whisked or sifted together before being mixed in stages into the batter. You can sift with an actual sifter, a gadget sold in any housewares department, or you can use a wire mesh strainer like I do. I prefer gadgets that have more than one use. There are two main reasons to sift the flour and other dry ingredients: One is to break up lumps (important for cocoa powder) and the other is to disperse minor ingredients, such as baking powder, evenly. If I am feeling proper, I'll actually dirty up a bowl and either sift all my dry ingredients or, at the very least, whisk them together. Most commonly, I hold the strainer over the bowl and sift directly onto the batter. It's lazy, for sure, but it works.

For delicate cakes, the liquids are added alternately with the flour, usually starting and ending with the flour mixture. Quick and efficient mixing ensures a cake that will be tender—overbeating develops the gluten protein too much and toughens the cake.

I am lackadaisical about mixing utensils. If the cake batter is on the thin side, I use an open, flimsy wire whisk to mix. I adore my collection of cheap wire whisks because they aerate efficiently and mix quickly but gently. If the batter is thick, I tend to beat it with a wooden spoon or silicone spatula. Oftentimes I use both whisk and spoon in the course of a recipe, since the consistency of the batter changes with the addition of more ingredients.

snack
cakes

Chocolate Fudge Snack Cake with Broiled Coconut-Pecan Topping

Super-moist with deep chocolate flavor, this is my favorite chocolate snacking cake. The coffee in the recipe accentuates the chocolate flavor, but the recipe will still work with plain warm water. If you want to make the cake even richer, fold ½ cup grated bittersweet chocolate into the batter before baking. Because I really adore cake, I usually eat it plain with a tall glass of ice-cold milk, but I've included a simple topping to jazz up the recipe. The Broiled Coconut-Pecan Topping is rich, almost like a candy bar, and takes just a few minutes to make. Burnt Sugar Frosting (page 154) or White Chocolate Whipped Cream (page 226) are two quite different but equally tasty alternatives.

MAKES 12 SERVINGS.

CHOCOLATE FUDGE SNACK CAKE

10 Tbs. unsalted butter, soft
1⅔ C. sugar
2 large eggs, at room temperature
1 tsp. vanilla extract
½ tsp. salt
1½ C. plus 2 Tbs. all-purpose flour

½ C. plus ⅓ C. unsweetened
   cocoa powder
1 tsp. baking soda
1 tsp. baking powder
1½ C. strong brewed coffee, cooled
   to just warm

BROILED COCONUT-PECAN TOPPING

3 Tbs. unsalted butter, at room
   temperature
¾ C. packed light brown sugar
¼ C. heavy whipping cream

1½ C. sweetened flaked coconut
⅔ C. finely chopped pecans
¼ C. mini semisweet chocolate chips

Preheat the oven to 350°F. Butter and flour a 9"-square baking pan. In a medium bowl, beat together the butter and sugar until smooth, about 1 minute. Whisk in the eggs, one at a time, until each is incorporated. Continue whisking until the batter is smooth, about another 30 seconds. Whisk in the vanilla and salt. Sift the flour, cocoa, baking soda, and baking powder directly onto the batter. Pour in the coffee. Gently whisk until smooth and mostly lump free. Pour the batter into the pan, spreading evenly with a spatula. Bake until a skewer inserted near the center comes out with only moist crumbs clinging, 40 to 43 minutes.

After you remove the cake from the oven, preheat the broiler, positioning the rack about 4" from the heat source. Prepare the frosting. In a medium bowl, beat together the butter and brown sugar until smooth. Beat in the cream. Stir in the coconut, pecans, and chocolate chips until well combined. Spread the mixture evenly over the top of the warm cake. Broil for 2 to 3 minutes or until bubbly and nicely browned. Cool the cake completely in the pan on a wire rack. Cut into 12 rectangles.

Cranberry Upside-Down Cake

A lot of upside-down cake recipes offer a delicious caramelized fruit over a dense, sturdy cake, but that's just not my cup of tea. I want my cake to be moist, tender, and buttery—the perfect foil for tart fruit like cranberries. If cranberries aren't available, use whatever fruit is in season—halved and pitted fresh cherries or apricots, pineapple slices, or thinly sliced apples or pears. This cake is best served the day it is made, preferably within an hour of coming out of the oven. Though it's commonly served for dessert (with ice cream), I also serve it for brunch.

MAKES 12 SERVINGS.

1 C. unsalted butter, soft (divided)

1 C. packed light brown sugar

¼ tsp. ground cinnamon

2 C. fresh or thawed frozen cranberries

1 C. sugar

1 large egg yolk, at room temperature

2 large eggs, at room temperature

⅔ C. sour cream, at room temperature

1 tsp. vanilla extract

½ tsp. salt

1¾ C. cake flour

1 tsp. baking powder

¼ tsp. baking soda

Preheat the oven to 350°F with a rack in the lower third of the oven. Butter the sides of a round cake pan 9" in diameter and at least 2" tall. Place ¼ cup of the butter in the pan. Heat in the oven until the butter melts, about 3 minutes. Remove from the oven and sprinkle evenly with the brown sugar and cinnamon. Sprinkle the cranberries over the sugar. Set aside.

In a medium bowl, beat the remaining ¾ cup of butter, the sugar, and the egg yolk until blended, about 20 seconds. Whisk in the whole eggs, one at a time. Whisk until the batter is smooth, about 30 seconds. Whisk in the sour cream, vanilla, and salt. Sift the cake flour, baking powder, and baking soda directly onto the batter. Whisk until smooth and lump free. Spread the batter evenly over the cranberry mixture in the pan.

Bake until the center of the cake springs back when touched gently and a skewer inserted near the center comes out with only moist crumbs clinging, 50 to 55 minutes. Cool in the pan on a wire rack for 5 minutes. Run a knife around the edge of the pan to loosen the cake. Place a serving plate over the top of the cake; invert the cake pan to unmold onto the plate. Let cool at least 15 minutes before serving. Best served warm.

Sweet Potato Cake with Pecan Streusel

You can use canned sweet potatoes for this moist cake, but a freshly baked sweet potato will deliver a more intense flavor and a fluffier texture. I like to roast my sweet potatoes at a high temperature, with a pan set on the oven rack beneath the potatoes to catch the caramelized syrup that drips off them as they approach perfect doneness—just soft enough to mash easily with a fork. Let the potatoes cool to just warm before you handle them. Pumpkin lovers can substitute 1 cup canned pumpkin puree for the sweet potato. Yes, I have a double standard—rarely have I encountered a home-baked pumpkin that delivered superior flavor to canned puree. But, by all means, roast your own pumpkin or squash if you like. Look for a variety called sugar pumpkin, which is a great variety for baking. Another hint—choose small, heavy pumpkins for the richest flavor.

MAKES 12 SERVINGS.

PECAN STREUSEL

⅔ C. all-purpose flour

½ C. packed light brown sugar

½ C. toasted chopped pecans

⅛ tsp. salt

¼ C. unsalted butter, melted

CAKE

¾ C. oil

1½ C. packed light brown sugar

3 large eggs, at room temperature

1 C. baked mashed sweet potato, at room temperature or just warm (from 1 large or 2 small sweet potatoes)

1 Tbs. molasses

1 Tbs. finely grated fresh ginger

¾ tsp. salt

¼ tsp. ground cinnamon

¼ tsp. ground cardamom

⅛ tsp. freshly grated nutmeg

1⅔ C. all-purpose flour

1½ tsp. baking soda

For the streusel, in a small bowl stir together the flour, brown sugar, pecans, and salt. Drizzle in the butter and stir until well combined. Squeeze the mixture between your fingers to form small clumps; set aside.

For the cake, preheat the oven to 350°F. Butter and flour a 9"-square baking pan. In a medium bowl, whisk together the oil, brown sugar, and eggs until smooth and creamy, about 1 minute. Whisk in the sweet potato, molasses, ginger, salt, cinnamon, cardamom, and nutmeg. Sift the flour and baking soda directly onto the batter. Using a whisk or rubber spatula, combine the ingredients until well-blended and almost smooth.

Pour the batter into the pan, spreading evenly with the spatula. Sprinkle the streusel evenly over the batter. Bake until a skewer inserted near the center comes out with only moist crumbs clinging, about 45 minutes. Cool until just warm in the pan on a wire rack. Cut into rectangles.

Chocolate Chip–Banana Snack Cake

This cake is one of life's simple pleasures. Exceptionally soft, moist, and fluffy, this little snack cake is a must for banana lovers. It's my first-choice recipe if I find myself with overripe bananas. It's also a great "first cake to bake" recipe for kids, because it always turns out well.

MAKES 9 SERVINGS.

1¼ C. mashed bananas (about 3 small or 2 medium)
1 C. sugar
½ C. unsalted butter, soft, or ½ C. oil
2 large eggs, at room temperature
½ tsp. vanilla extract

1 C. all-purpose flour
¼ C. cake flour
1 tsp. baking soda
½ tsp. salt
½ C. mini semisweet chocolate chips

Preheat the oven to 350°F. Butter and flour an 8"-square baking pan. In a large bowl, whisk together the bananas, sugar, and butter or oil until well combined, about 1 minute. Whisk in the eggs, one at time, and the vanilla until the batter is smooth and creamy. (There may be some banana lumps remaining and that is just fine.) Sift the flours, baking soda, and salt directly over the batter. Quickly and gently stir in the dry ingredients until just barely incorporated. Before all the flour is fully mixed into the batter, sprinkle the chocolate chips into the bowl and stir until just incorporated. Do not overmix. Bake for 33 to 35 minutes or until a skewer inserted near center of the cake comes out with only moist crumbs clinging. Cool in the pan on a wire rack for 20 minutes before serving. Cut into squares.

Apple Cake with Caramel Sauce

This cake falls under the category of autumn comfort food. I serve it warm, with caramel sauce or ice cream. It's a homely cake, with a mottled top and crispy edges, but it's wonderfully moist inside. This recipe is adapted from the Junior League cookbook *A Taste of Oregon*. Chris Ritter, a dear family friend and home cook extraordinaire, introduced me to it a few years ago. I had tried all manner of apple cake recipes, but this one is my favorite. The original recipe uses shortening, which makes a light, fine-textured cake. I like the flavor of butter with apples, so I've split the difference. I've altered the spices a bit to include nutmeg and cloves, which I also love with apples, and since I am partial to smoky, dark caramel sauces, I've made my own.

MAKES 15 SERVINGS.

APPLE CAKE

½ C. unsalted butter, soft

½ C. shortening

2 C. sugar

2 large eggs, at room temperature

4 C. finely chopped (¼" to ½" pieces) peeled tart baking apples, such as Pink Lady, Golden Delicious, Braeburn, or Granny Smith (about 3 medium apples)

1¼ C. all-purpose flour

¾ C. cake flour

2 tsp. baking soda

1 tsp. ground cinnamon

½ tsp. salt

¼ tsp. freshly grated nutmeg

Pinch of ground cloves

½ C. toasted chopped pecans or walnuts

Preheat the oven to 350°F. Butter and flour a 13" x 9" cake pan. In a large bowl, beat the butter, shortening, and sugar until smooth and fluffy, about 2 minutes. One at time, whisk in the eggs until the mixture is smooth and creamy. Stir in the apples. Sift the flours, baking soda, cinnamon, salt, nutmeg, and cloves directly over the batter and gently and quickly fold them in until just combined. Scrape the batter into the pan and smooth gently with a spatula. Sprinkle the toasted nuts across the top. Bake for 40 minutes or until a skewer inserted near the center of the cake comes out clean. After removing from the oven, run a knife or metal spatula around the edge of the cake to loosen it from the pan. Cool in the pan on a wire rack for 20 minutes before serving. Cut into rectangles. Serve drizzled with the caramel sauce.

CARAMEL SAUCE

MAKES ABOUT 2 CUPS SAUCE.

1⅓ C. sugar

⅔ C. warm water

1½ C. heavy whipping cream

1 Tbs. unsalted butter

¼ tsp. salt

Pour the sugar in an even layer into a medium, heavy saucepan set over medium heat; sprinkle with the water. Stir occasionally or swirl the pan to encourage the sugar to melt. When the sugar has melted (this will take about 2 minutes), increase the heat to medium-high. Watch the bubbling sugar syrup carefully. After a minute or two, the sugar should start to caramelize. As the edges turn golden, gently swirl the pan (but do not stir the syrup directly) for even caramelization. Continue to let the syrup cook until it is a deep amber color—a pale gold syrup will not make a flavorful sauce base. Turn off the heat and carefully add the cream and butter to the pan—it will rise and foam dramatically. Stir in the salt. Continue to stir until the mixture is smooth. If the mixture forms hard lumps when the cream is added, simply reheat over low heat until melted. The caramel may be made ahead and stored in the refrigerator; simply reheat when ready to use.

Chocolate Cupcakes with Burnt Sugar Frosting

Cupcakes aren't just for kids anymore, as one bite of these cakes will tell you. I love the burnt sugar frosting with them, which is similar in flavor to old-fashioned penuche frostings made with brown sugar. The Fudge Frosting (page 169) is a nice alternative. Notice that the baking soda is dissolved in liquid before being mixed into the batter, which greatly diminishes its capacity to leaven the cake. The baking soda's function here is not to leaven, but to alter the pH (acidity) of the batter. Baking soda is an alkaline agent, and by adding it to the cocoa and liquid, we alkalize the chocolate, adjusting its flavor and changing the finished grain of the cake. There is little baking powder in the recipe, just enough to give a light rise and keep the crumb very fine. Classic devil's food cake has more leavening, especially soda, which gives it a more open-crumb grain.

MAKES 1 DOZEN CUPCAKES.

CHOCOLATE CUPCAKES

½ C. unsweetened cocoa powder

½ tsp. baking soda

¾ C. warm (not hot) brewed coffee
    or water

10 Tbs. unsalted butter, soft

¾ C. sugar

1 large egg, at room temperature

1 tsp. vanilla extract

¼ tsp. salt

1 C. all-purpose flour

½ tsp. baking powder

Preheat the oven to 350°F. Line 12 standard cupcake cups with foil or paper liners. Place the cocoa and baking soda in a small bowl; slowly whisk in the coffee or warm water until smooth. In a medium bowl, beat the butter and sugar until smooth and fluffy, about 1 minute. Whisk in the egg, vanilla, and salt until the batter is smooth, about 30 seconds. Sift the flour with the baking powder; stir half the flour mixture into the batter. Stir in all of the chocolate liquid, then finish by stirring in the remaining flour mixture. The batter should be smooth, but do not overbeat. Divide the batter evenly among the cupcake liners. Bake for 15 to 17 minutes or until a skewer inserted near the center of a cupcake comes out with very moist crumbs clinging.

BURNT SUGAR FROSTING

12 Tbs. cold unsalted butter (divided)	½ tsp. salt
3 Tbs. corn syrup	⅓ C. heavy whipping cream
¾ C. packed light brown sugar	

In a small, heavy pan, melt 3 tablespoons of the butter with the corn syrup over medium-high heat. Stir in the brown sugar and salt and cook, stirring occasionally, for 5 to 6 minutes. (The mixture will darken at the edges and become fragrant as it caramelizes; a candy thermometer will register 260°F when inserted into the center of the liquid.) Remove the pan from the heat; let sit for 1 minute. Carefully stir in the cream. Let the pan sit for 10 minutes. One at a time, whisk in the remaining 9 tablespoons cold butter. Scrape the mixture into a bowl and let cool. When cool, whisk the frosting until thick, fluffy, and spreadable. You can chill the mixture in the refrigerator to accelerate the process. Frost each cupcake with about 3 tablespoons of the frosting. If your kitchen is warm, store the frosted cupcakes in the refrigerator.

Walnut-Topped Banana Cupcakes with Maple Frosting

This simple variation of banana bread makes a perfect breakfast or school snack. Maple and lightly toasted walnuts are great flavors with banana. Bake the batter in a loaf pan if cupcakes aren't your thing.

MAKES 1 DOZEN CUPCAKES.

BANANA CUPCAKES

½ C. oil

1 C. sugar

2 large eggs, at room temperature

1¼ C. mashed bananas (about 3)

2 C. all-purpose flour

2 tsp. baking powder

½ tsp. baking soda

½ tsp. salt

⅓ C. buttermilk or plain yogurt, at room temperature

MAPLE FROSTING

4 Tbs. cream cheese, very soft

2 Tbs. unsalted butter, soft

½ tsp. vanilla extract

½ tsp. maple flavoring

Pinch of salt

1½ C. powdered sugar

TOPPING

¼ cup lightly toasted chopped walnuts

For the cupcakes, preheat the oven to 350°F. Line 12 standard cupcake cups with foil or paper liners. In a large bowl, whisk together the oil, sugar, and eggs until light and fluffy, about 2 minutes. Lightly whisk in the banana. Sift together the flour, baking powder, baking soda, and salt. Add half of the dry ingredients to the banana mixture, stirring until just combined. Stir in all of the buttermilk or yogurt until just combined and then the remaining dry ingredients. Divide the batter evenly among the cupcake liners. Bake for 16 to 18 minutes or until a tester inserted near the center of a cupcake comes out with only moist crumbs clinging. Cool the cupcakes completely out of the pan on a wire rack.

For the maple frosting, in a medium bowl, beat together the cream cheese, butter, vanilla, maple flavoring, and salt until smooth. Gradually beat in the powdered sugar, about ¼ cup at time, until the frosting is fluffy and spreadable, about 1 minute. Spread about 2 tablespoons of frosting on each cupcake and sprinkle with about 1 teaspoon of the chopped walnuts.

big
cakes

Chocolate Stout Cake

It may sound strange, but the unusual combination of chocolate and stout makes for a great cake. I like to use a chocolate stout if I can find one, but any stout will do. The molasses makes the cake very moist—this cake will keep for several days and is great for gift giving. If you like the combination of chocolate and gingerbread, stir in your favorite gingerbread spices, like cinnamon, ginger, clove, and/or nutmeg. The cake is wonderful served plain with a dusting of powdered sugar, but a glaze of chocolate ganache makes it a real winner.

MAKES 16 SERVINGS.

1¼ C. stout, such as Guinness (do not include foam when measuring)

⅓ C. dark molasses

1¼ C. unsalted butter, soft

1½ C. packed light brown sugar

3 large eggs, at room temperature

1⅔ C. all-purpose flour

¾ C. unsweetened natural cocoa powder, plus more for the pan

1½ tsp. baking powder

½ tsp. baking soda

½ tsp. salt

6 oz. semisweet chocolate, very finely chopped

CHOCOLATE GANACHE GLAZE (OPTIONAL)

¾ C. heavy cream

6 oz. semisweet chocolate, chopped

Preheat the oven to 350°F. Butter a 12-cup Bundt pan and dust with cocoa powder. Tap out excess cocoa. For the cake, in a small saucepan over high heat, bring the stout and molasses to a simmer. Remove from the heat; reserve. In a large bowl, beat together the butter and brown sugar until smooth, about 2 minutes. Whisk in the eggs, one at a time, until each is incorporated. Continue whisking until the batter is smooth, about another 30 seconds. In another bowl, whisk together the flour, cocoa, baking powder, baking soda, and salt. Add the flour and stout mixtures alternately to the butter mixture, beginning and ending with the flour and stirring to incorporate each addition, about 30 seconds per addition. Stir in the chopped chocolate. Spread the batter into the pan, rapping it on the counter to level and eliminate any air pockets. Bake for 45 to 50 minutes or until a skewer inserted near the center comes out with only moist crumbs clinging. Cool in the pan on a wire rack for 20 minutes. Invert the cake onto the rack to unmold. Let cool until just barely warm.

For the chocolate glaze, if desired, bring the cream to a boil in a small saucepan over high heat. Remove the pan from the heat; add the chocolate. Let stand for 1 minute and then whisk until smooth. Cool for 5 minutes and then drizzle over the cake.

Orange–Poppy Seed Pound Cake

Cream cheese is the secret ingredient in this cake, adding a moist texture that is smooth and fine. To make the cake easier to mix by hand, be sure to start with room-temperature cream cheese. If your poppy seeds have lost their aroma, simply toss them in a warm skillet until fragrant. This recipe makes two loaves, leaving you an extra for sharing or to keep on hand in the freezer.

MAKES 16 SERVINGS.

CAKE

1½ C. unsalted butter, soft

1 (8-oz.) pkg. cream cheese, soft

2½ C. sugar

4 tsp. grated orange zest

6 large eggs, at room temperature

2 large egg yolks, at room temperature

1 tsp. vanilla extract

2⅔ C. all-purpose flour

1½ tsp. baking powder

½ tsp. salt

⅓ C. poppy seeds

ORANGE GLAZE

⅔ C. fresh orange juice

⅓ C. sugar

1 Tbs. orange liqueur, such as Cointreau

Preheat the oven to 350°F. Butter and flour two 9" x 5" loaf pans. In a medium bowl, beat the butter, cream cheese, sugar, and orange zest until light and fluffy, 2 to 3 minutes. Beat in the eggs, one by one, and then the egg yolks and the vanilla—about 1½ minutes for all or until the batter is smooth and creamy. Sift the flour, baking powder, and salt directly over the batter and stir to just incorporate. Stir in the poppy seeds. Divide the batter between the two loaf pans and rap them on the counter to eliminate any air pockets. Bake for 50 minutes or until a skewer inserted in the center comes out with only moist crumbs clinging. Cool in the pans on a wire rack for 10 minutes. Remove the cakes from the pans and brush with the glaze while still warm.

For the Orange Glaze, in a small saucepan bring the orange juice to a boil over high heat. Stir in the sugar and cook until the liquid is reduced to a scant ½ cup, 3 to 4 minutes. Remove from the heat and stir in the liqueur. Brush the tops and sides of the cakes with the glaze, repeating every few minutes until all the glaze has been used. Let the cakes cool completely before wrapping.

Everyone loves a moist carrot cake, and this simple version baked in a Bundt pan is perfect for everyday baking. It stays moist for days, and the flavor is actually best the day after it's made. I just love a carrot cake baked as a ring cake—it's so much easier to eat out of hand, and far less rich without the mountains of frosting and filling that usually adorn layer cakes. I've included a recipe for a lightly sweetened cream cheese spread that lets you have just enough creamy goodness without making the cake cloyingly sweet.

MAKES 16 SERVINGS.

1⅓ C. cake flour

1 C. all-purpose flour

1½ tsp. baking powder

1½ tsp. baking soda

1 tsp. ground ginger

1 tsp. ground cinnamon

½ tsp. salt

1½ C. packed light brown sugar

3 large eggs, at room temperature

1 C. mayonnaise (not salad dressing)

2 C. shredded carrots (about 2 large)

1 (8 oz.) can crushed pineapple, well drained

¾ C. toasted chopped walnuts (optional)

Preheat the oven to 350°F. Butter and flour a 12-cup Bundt pan. Whisk together the flours, baking powder, baking soda, spices, and salt; set aside. Place the sugar in a large bowl. Beat in one egg at a time, pressing the lumps out of the sugar (this is easiest without all the eggs added in at once). Beat for 30 seconds after each egg is added, and then beat in the mayonnaise. Stir in the carrots and the pineapple until well combined. Stir in the dry ingredients and the nuts, if desired—do not overmix at this point. Spread the batter into the prepared pan. Bake for 44 to 47 minutes or until a skewer inserted near the center of the cake comes out with only moist crumbs clinging. Cool for 15 minutes in the pan on a wire rack; invert the cake onto the rack to cool completely.

Gingered Cream Cheese Spread

I love cream cheese frosting, and this spread is a less-sweet version perfect for spreading over individual slices of the carrot cake. I've added a bit of crystal- lized ginger and fresh citrus zest to the spread for extra punch, but you can serve it plain, too. This recipe may be doubled for folks who like to heap their cake with cream cheese. If you make it ahead, be sure to let it stand at room temperature for 15 to 20 minutes so it's easy to spread. Try it with moist Zuc- chini Bread (page 65), too.

MAKES ⅔ CUP.

4 oz. (half of an 8-oz. pkg.) cream
   cheese, soft
2 Tbs. unsalted butter, soft
¼ C. powdered sugar

½ tsp. grated orange zest or 1 tsp.
   grated lemon zest
2 Tbs. finely minced crystallized
   ginger

In a small bowl, beat together the cream cheese and the butter until smooth. Beat in the sugar gradually, a tablespoon or so at time. Beat in the zest and the ginger and continue beating until fluffy, about another minute.

Marble Bundt Cake

Marble cakes are made by taking a portion of a plain vanilla batter and stirring in another flavor, in this case chocolate. Most recipes have you simply add cocoa powder to the plain batter, but that can make the chocolate portion of the cake seem dry and not truly chocolaty. I make a thin paste of cocoa and milk, to which I add a little grated chocolate to ensure moist richness. A fine dusting of powdered sugar is the only garnish needed, but chocoholics may wish to pour Chocolate Ganache Glaze (page 159) over the cake for an over-the-top experience.

MAKES 16 SERVINGS.

1 C. milk, at room temperature (divided)	2½ C. all-purpose flour
1 tsp. vanilla extract	2½ tsp. baking powder
⅓ C. unsweetened cocoa powder	1 C. plus 2 Tbs. unsalted butter, soft
2 oz. semisweet or bittersweet chocolate, grated	2 C. sugar
	½ tsp. salt
	4 large eggs, at room temperature

Preheat the oven to 350°F. Butter and flour a 12-cup Bundt pan. Combine the milk and the vanilla. In a small bowl, whisk the cocoa with ¼ cup of the milk until no lumps remain. Stir the grated chocolate into the cocoa mixture. In another bowl, whisk together the flour and the baking powder. In a large bowl, beat the butter, sugar, and salt together until smooth and fluffy, about 2 minutes. One at a time, beat in the eggs. Stir in the flour in three additions, alternating with the remaining milk, but starting and ending with the flour. Stir approximately one-third of the batter into the chocolate mixture until no pale streaks remain. Dollop some white batter into the bottom of the pan, alternating dollops of chocolate batter. Repeat until both batters are finished. Rap the pan on the counter to eliminate any air pockets. Bake for 45 to 47 minutes or until a skewer inserted near the center comes out with only moist crumbs clinging. Cool in the pan on a wire rack for 20 minutes. Cool completely out of the pan on the rack.

Moist Vanilla Pound Cake, Plus Five Variations

Historically, the true recipe for pound cake is equal parts (by weight) butter, sugar, eggs, and flour. That's it—so easy you don't even have to write it down. Trouble is, the traditional recipe just doesn't suit our modern tastes—it makes a cake that seems too dense, hard, and a bit dry, with a pronounced eggy flavor. To update the classic recipe, I've increased the sugar (for tenderness) and added milk (for moisture), while reducing the amount of egg (to decrease dryness). I've also added baking powder for a foolproof rise and a fine crumb. You won't get the high, peaked top associated with old-fashioned pound cakes, but you'll love the texture and flavor. And as you can see, the basic recipe is easy to vary.

MAKES 16 SERVINGS.

¾ C. milk, at room temperature
1 tsp. vanilla extract
2½ C. all-purpose flour
2½ tsp. baking powder

1 C. plus 2 Tbs. unsalted butter, soft
1¾ C. sugar
½ tsp. salt
4 large eggs, at room temperature

Preheat the oven to 350°F. Butter and flour a 12-cup Bundt pan. Combine the milk and the vanilla. In a medium bowl, whisk together the flour and the baking powder. In a large bowl, beat the butter, sugar, and salt together until smooth and fluffy, about 2 minutes. One at a time, beat in the eggs. Stir in the flour in three additions, alternating with the milk, but starting and ending with the flour. Gently spread the batter into the prepared baking pan. Bake for 42 to 45 minutes or until a skewer inserted near the center comes out with only moist crumbs clinging. Cool in the pan on a wire rack for 20 minutes. Cool completely out of the pan on the rack.

Variations on next page.

→ **BLUEBERRY POUND CAKE:** Stir 1½ cups fresh blueberries into the batter and increase the baking time by 5 minutes.

→ **EGGNOG POUND CAKE WITH SPIKED GLAZE:** Stir ½ teaspoon freshly grated nutmeg into the completed batter. For the glaze, combine 1¼ cups powdered sugar with 3 tablespoons each brandy and rum. After 15 minutes of cooling, invert the warm cake onto a serving plate. Using a skewer, poke holes all over the cake. Brush every inch of visible cake with the glaze until the glaze is gone. When the cake is completely cool, the glaze will form a protective crust over the cake.

→ **ALMOND, LEMON, AND COCONUT POUND CAKE WITH LEMON GLAZE:** Reduce the milk to ½ cup, and add ¼ cup lemon juice. Stir ½ teaspoon almond extract into the milk. Stir 1 tablespoon grated lemon zest and 1 cup loosely packed sweetened flaked coconut into the batter, breaking up any lumps. For the glaze, combine 1¼ cups powdered sugar with ½ cup fresh lemon juice. After 15 minutes of cooling, invert the warm cake onto a serving plate. Using a skewer, poke holes all over the cake. Brush every inch of visible cake with the glaze until the glaze is gone. When the cake is completely cool, the glaze will form a protective crust over the cake.

→ **CRANBERRY–WALNUT STREUSEL POUND CAKE:** Reduce the milk in the batter to ½ cup. In a small bowl, combine ⅔ cup lightly toasted chopped walnut pieces, ½ cup packed brown sugar, and ½ teaspoon ground cinnamon. Have at the ready 1 cup fresh or thawed chopped cranberries.

Spoon one-quarter of the batter into the bottom of the prepared Bundt pan—enough to make a thin layer. Sprinkle ⅓ cup of the cranberries over the batter, then a scant third of the walnut streusel on top of the berries. Spoon half the remaining batter over this layer, then half the cranberries and walnut streusel over the batter. Repeat one more time, finishing with the streusel. Increase the baking time by 5 minutes.

→ **CHOCOLATE CHIP POUND CAKE:** Reduce the milk to ⅔ cup and stir 1 cup mini semisweet chocolate chips into the batter.

Ganache-Filled Chocolate Layer Cake with Caramel Whipped Cream Frosting

I've never been a fan of heavy frostings that overwhelm the delicate texture of a really good cake, so I've covered this rich devil's food–style chocolate cake with a fluffy whipped cream frosting instead. Making the caramel sauce for the frosting is the trickiest part of the recipe, but the wonderful flavor is worth the effort. I find it easiest to assemble the cake and filling before I make the Caramel Whipped Cream. The frosting sets up as it cools, so it's smooth and easier to spread right after it's made. If you like the flavor of peanut butter, stir ⅓ cup into the warm caramel sauce for a nutty variation.

MAKES 12 SERVINGS.

CHOCOLATE CAKE LAYERS

1½ C. all-purpose flour
⅔ C. unsweetened cocoa powder
1½ tsp. baking powder
½ tsp. baking soda
½ tsp. salt

1½ C. sugar
½ C. oil
2 large eggs, at room temperature
1⅓ C. warm water (or brewed coffee)

GANACHE FILLING

¾ C. heavy whipping cream

4 oz. bittersweet chocolate, chopped

CARAMEL WHIPPED CREAM FROSTING

1 C. packed light brown sugar
¼ C. water
4 Tbs. unsalted butter (divided)

⅛ tsp. salt
2 C. heavy whipping cream (divided)

CHOCOLATE CURLS (OPTIONAL)

2 oz. bittersweet chocolate, shaved
    into curls using a vegetable peeler

For the Chocolate Cake Layers, preheat the oven to 350°F. Butter and flour two 9"-round cake pans. Sift together the flour, cocoa, baking powder, baking soda, and salt. In a large bowl, beat the sugar, oil, and eggs until light and fluffy, about 2 minutes. Alternately add the flour mixture and the water or coffee to the sugar mixture, starting and finishing with the flour. Divide the batter evenly between the pans. Bake for 23 to 25 minutes or until the top springs back when pressed and a skewer inserted near the center comes out with only moist crumbs clinging. Cool in the pans on a wire rack for 15 to 20 minutes. Remove the cakes from the pans and cool completely.

For the Ganache Filling, in a small saucepan over high heat, bring the cream to a boil. Remove the pan from the heat and add the chopped chocolate. Let stand for 1 minute; stir until smooth. Let cool to spreading consistency, about 30 minutes at room temperature.

To assemble the cake, trim one of the cake layers to level the top if necessary and place on a serving plate. Spread with the Ganache Filling and top with the remaining cake layer, domed side up. Refrigerate until set.

Meanwhile, for the Caramel Whipped Cream Frosting, in a medium, heavy skillet over medium-high heat, stir together the brown sugar, water, 2 tablespoons of the butter, and the salt until dissolved. Bring to a boil. Cover and boil for 2 minutes, letting the steam wash down the sides of the pan. Uncover and cook for another 1 to 2 minutes without stirring until the temperature reaches 260°F. The mixture will darken at the edges and become fragrant as it caramelizes. Tilt the pan to swirl the caramel and ensure even caramelization. Remove the pan from the heat and stir in the remaining butter and ½ cup of the heavy cream. Pour into a large bowl and let cool until just barely warm—almost room temperature. If it thickens so it won't pour, add a bit of warm water to loosen. Beat the remaining heavy cream to soft peaks. Fold a quarter of the whipped cream into the caramel to lighten it. Gently fold in the remaining whipped cream.

To frost, spread the top and sides of the assembled chilled cake with the Caramel Whipped Cream. Chill until set. If desired, garnish with chocolate curls. Let stand for 10 to 15 minutes before serving.

Chocolate Layer Cake with Fudge Frosting

If you want to win friends and influence people, serve them this cake. This fudge frosting is my all-time favorite—it's creamy and rich but not at all too sweet. And because it starts with caramel sauce, the flavor notes are smoky and complex. Seriously, this is the sort of cake that will get you a marriage proposal. For the best texture, don't refrigerate the cake at all, just leave it on the counter. You don't even need to wrap the uncut cake—the fudge frosting will keep the tender cake perfectly sealed.

MAKES 16 SERVINGS.

2 baked Chocolate Cake Layers
   (page 167)

FUDGE FROSTING

12 Tbs. unsalted butter (divided)
1 C. packed light brown sugar
¼ C. light corn syrup
¼ tsp. salt
1 C. heavy whipping cream

1 oz. unsweetened chocolate, finely
   chopped
7 oz. bittersweet chocolate, finely
   chopped
2 tsp. vanilla extract

In a medium, heavy saucepan over medium heat, melt 6 tablespoons of the butter. Add the brown sugar, the corn syrup, and the salt and stir until dissolved. Bring the mixture to a boil. Boil for 5 to 6 minutes without stirring until the mixture reaches 260°F, swirling the mixture in the pan to ensure even caramelization as it darkens at the edges. Remove from the heat and stir in the cream (the mixture will bubble up) until smooth. Add the chocolates and the vanilla and whisk until smooth and melted. Whisk in the remaining butter. Transfer the frosting to a bowl and let it sit at room temperature until no longer hot, 20 to 30 minutes. Then refrigerate the bowl, whisking every 5 minutes or so, until the frosting thickens to spreading consistency, about 15 minutes.

Trim the domed top from one of the cake layers and place it on a serving plate. Spread with 1 cup of the Fudge Frosting. Top with the remaining cake layer. Spread the remaining frosting over the top and sides of the cake. This makes about 3½ cups frosting, enough for an ample covering on the top and sides of the cake, plus some additional to pipe on as decoration.

The contrast of creamy vanilla custard against satiny, dark chocolate glaze makes for one of the best combinations in cake history. For the cake to be truly perfect, though, a sponge cake is a must for the base. I've used a chiffon cake here, both airy and light—the perfect foil for a rich filling. Chiffon cake, unlike regular layer cake, is tender when cold, great even straight out of the refrigerator. This is important because we've essentially put vanilla pudding between the layers, which would ooze out if left at room temperature for too long. You can divide the batter between two 8" or 9" pans or bake it all in one large 10"-round pan that you'll cut in half horizontally after the cake is baked. Because a sponge cake is heavy on eggs and light on flour, it'll shrink back a bit as it cools—this is normal, and unless the cake loses more than 25 percent of its volume, you've done nothing wrong.

MAKES 8 SERVINGS.

CHIFFON CAKE LAYERS

1 C. cake flour
¾ C. sugar (divided)
1 tsp. baking powder
½ tsp. salt

4 large eggs, separated
¼ C. oil
⅓ C. warm milk or hot water
¾ tsp. vanilla extract

½ recipe (a generous 1⅓ cups) Bourbon Vanilla Pastry Cream (page 225)

Chocolate Glaze (page 80)

Preheat the oven to 350°F. Butter and flour only the bottom of two 9" x 2" round cake pans. In a large bowl, whisk together the flour, ¼ cup sugar, the baking powder, and the salt until smooth. Whisk in the egg yolks and the oil to make a smooth paste, adding some of the milk if necessary. Whisk in the remaining milk and the vanilla. In a medium bowl, beat the egg whites with a clean whisk until they form soft peaks, 2 to 3 minutes. Beat in the remaining sugar, in three or four additions, beating for 20 seconds after each addition. Continue to beat until the sugar granules dissolve and the whites hold soft peaks. Gently but quickly, fold the whites into the flour mixture in two additions.

Divide the batter evenly between the prepared pans. Bake for 20 to 25 minutes, until the center is set on the top and springs back to the touch or a skewer inserted near the center comes out clean. Cool in the pans on a wire rack for 10 minutes. Cool completely out of the pans on the wire rack.

Trim the domed top from one of the cake layers and place it on a serving plate. Spread with the Bourbon Vanilla Pastry Cream and top with the remaining cake layer. Reheat the Chocolate Glaze if necessary in a double boiler so it is pourable. Pour the glaze over the top of the assembled cake, using an offset spatula to spread to the edges and allowing it to drip over the sides.

Lemon Coconut Cloud Cake

This cake appeals to my inner grandma—an old southern woman who loves a good butter cake filled with super-tart lemon curd and topped with a cloud of lemon-scented whipped cream. Oh yes, and don't forget the coconut. This festive cake is wonderful for both winter and spring celebrations.

MAKES 12 SERVINGS.

LEMON CAKE LAYERS

2½ C. cake flour

2 tsp. baking powder

½ tsp. baking soda

½ tsp. salt

1 C. plus 2 Tbs. unsalted butter, soft

1⅔ C. sugar

2 tsp. grated lemon zest

2 large eggs, at room temperature

2 large egg yolks, at room temperature

¾ C. milk, at room temperature

¼ C. freshly squeezed lemon juice

1 recipe Lemon Curd (page 227; divided)

1 C. sweetened flaked coconut, lightly toasted (divided)

1 recipe White Chocolate Whipped Cream (page 226)

Preheat the oven to 350°F. Butter and flour two 9"-round cake pans. Sift together the cake flour, baking powder, baking soda, and salt. In a large bowl, beat the butter, sugar, and lemon zest until light and fluffy, about 2 minutes. One at a time, beat in the eggs and then the egg yolks, beating for about 20 seconds after each addition. Alternately add the flour mixture and the milk, starting and finishing with the flour. Stir in the lemon juice until just combined. Divide the batter evenly between the pans. Bake for 25 to 30 minutes or until the top springs back when pressed and a skewer inserted near the center comes out with only moist crumbs clinging. Cool in the pans on a wire rack for 15 to 20 minutes. Remove the cakes from the pans and cool completely.

To assemble the cake, trim the domed top from one of the cake layers and place on a serving plate. Spread with 1¼ cups of the Lemon Curd and sprinkle with ⅓ cup coconut. Top with the remaining cake layer. Fold the remaining Lemon Curd into the White Chocolate Whipped Cream. Spread over the top and sides of the cake. Sprinkle the top and sides of the cake with the remaining coconut. If making ahead, refrigerate until ready to serve. Let the cake sit at room temperature for at least 15 minutes before slicing to let the cake warm up and become tender.

An American classic, this delicate butter cake is filled and topped with a rich, thick, fudgy frosting—the quintessential birthday cake. If you make this cake ahead and store it in the refrigerator, be sure to let the cake stand at room temperature for at least 40 minutes before serving to ensure the frosting and cake both soften. I prefer to leave the cake on the counter at room temperature—the fudgy frosting seals the interior perfectly. Butter-based layer cakes should never be served cold or they'll seem crumbly, hard, and dry. Not a nice thing to do to a perfectly nice cake, so let it warm up to show off its tender, delicate side.

MAKES 16 SERVINGS.

GOLDEN YELLOW CAKE LAYERS

2½ C. cake flour

2 tsp. baking powder

½ tsp. salt

1 C. plus 2 Tbs. unsalted butter, soft

1⅔ C. sugar

2 large eggs, at room temperature

2 large egg yolks, at room temperature

1 C. milk

2 tsp. vanilla extract

1 recipe Fudge Frosting (page 169)

Preheat the oven to 350°F. Butter and flour two 9"-round cake pans. Sift together the cake flour, baking powder, and salt. In a large bowl, beat the butter and sugar until light and fluffy, about 2 minutes. One at a time, beat in the eggs and then the egg yolks, beating for about 20 seconds after each addition. Combine the milk and the vanilla. Alternately add the flour mixture and the milk, starting and finishing with the flour. Divide the batter evenly between the pans. Bake for 25 to 30 minutes or until the top springs back when pressed and a skewer inserted near the center comes out with only moist crumbs clinging. Cool in the pans on a wire rack for 15 to 20 minutes. Remove the cakes from the pans and cool completely.

Trim the domed top from one of the cake layers and place on a serving plate. Spread with 1 cup of the Fudge Frosting. Top with the remaining cake layer. Spread the remaining frosting over the top and sides of the cake.

Strawberries & Cream Cake

This is the perfect cake for celebrating spring, and it's the cake I request each year for my birthday. Two tender, golden yellow cake layers are filled with luscious pastry cream lightened with whipped cream and plenty of sliced ripe strawberries. The top of the cake is covered with more of the vanilla mousse and garnished with fresh berries. It's a casual cake that requires no decorating skills whatsoever, and yet it makes an irresistible centerpiece—sort of a like a formal strawberry shortcake. If you don't like to assemble cakes of any kind, you can slice the cake into cubes and serve the recipe as a berry trifle.

MAKES 12 SERVINGS.

1 pint fresh ripe strawberries
2 Tbs. sugar
⅔ C. heavy whipping cream
1 recipe Bourbon Vanilla Pastry
   Cream, cold (page 225)

1 recipe Golden Yellow Cake Layers
   (page 174)

Hull the strawberries and slice thinly. Sprinkle the sugar over the berries and let stand for 15 minutes. Meanwhile, beat the heavy cream in a chilled bowl with a chilled whisk until stiff peaks form. Fold the whipped cream into the Bourbon Vanilla Pastry Cream.

Trim the domed top from one of the cake layers and place on a serving plate. Cover evenly with about half the sliced berries, including their juices. Spread 1½ to 2 cups of the lightened pastry cream over the fruit, not quite to the edge as it will press out when top layer is put on. Top with the remaining cake layer. Spread the top of the cake with the remaining lightened pastry cream and spoon the remaining berries over the cream. Serve immediately.

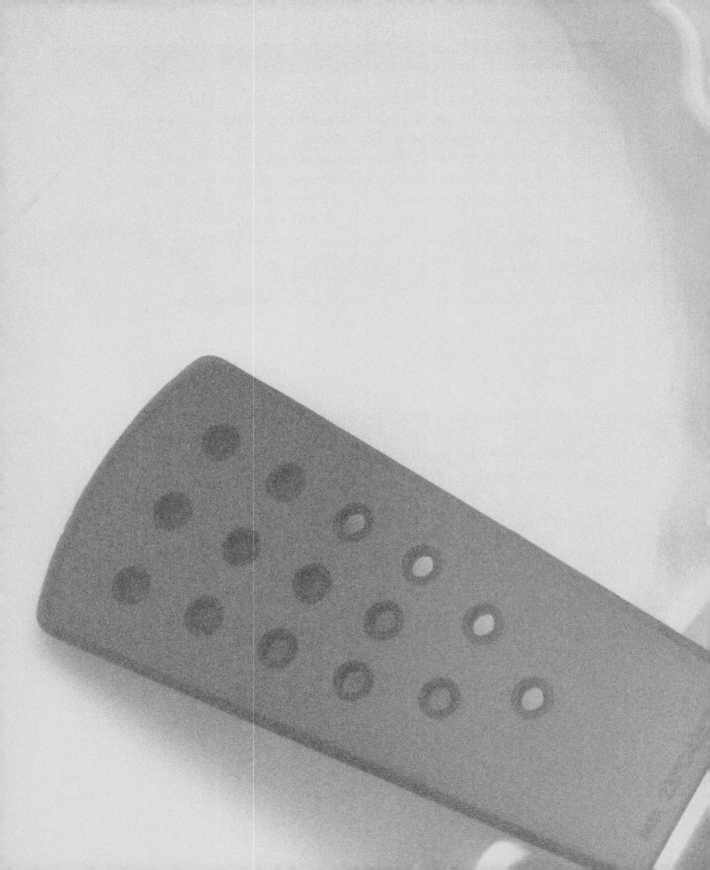

07

FRUIT PIES, FRUIT TARTS, & MORE

pies, tarts, cobblers, and crisps are the preferred desserts in my circle of family and friends. I think of them as being homey comfort food, and not the least bit special compared to a mousse or cake, but time and time again I watch guests pass by the cake for extra helpings of these. Maybe it's the wholesomeness of fresh fruit, or the way they don't seem overly sweet and heavy, but fruit desserts reign supreme.

Pie is truly the quintessential American dessert, and out of all the desserts you could make at home, I think it is the most rewarding and worthwhile. Why? Because you control the sweetness and spices, and home-baked pie pastry is crisper and more delicious than anything you can buy. Just be prepared: When your family and friends become accustomed to home-baked pie and fruity desserts at your house, you will be expected to produce them regularly for holidays and gatherings.

Since I make lots of pie, I don't really think of it as a bunch of different recipes, but more as a single formula with infinite variations: All I really need to know is how many cups of fruit fit into a pie shell and how much sugar and cornstarch to add. The types of fruit I combine, the spices I choose, and whether or not I choose a streusel topping are pure improvisation. If you are a pie-baking novice, here are a few tips and guidelines for making great pies every time.

Tips for Perfect Pies

Thawed frozen fruit can be used for any of these pies. Just be sure to measure the volume of the fruit while it's frozen—it will collapse dramatically as it thaws.

Fruit is variable in both sweetness and juiciness. If your fruit is especially tart or seems to throw off a lot of juice, you may need to increase the amount of sugar or cornstarch, respectively.

With the exception of apple pie, all of the fruit recipes in this chapter are thickened with cornstarch. Cornstarch-thickened pies have juices that are translucent, letting the color of the fruit shine through.

A pie isn't fully cooked until the juices near the center of the pie have thickened. Don't be fooled by bubbling juices at the edge of the pan—the edges will be done long before the rest of the pie. Watch for bubbling toward the center; otherwise the center will be too runny.

Make large batches of pie dough, shape it into disks, and freeze it to be pie-ready at a moment's notice.

Whole unbaked fruit pies may be frozen. You don't need to thaw them before baking—simply pop them into a hot oven. The baking time will be much longer—at least an extra 30 minutes. Metal pie tins are less cumbersome in your freezer than glass, and they transition more safely from the freezer to a preheated baking sheet.

For a super-crisp crust, chill the assembled pie before baking, and bake it on a preheated baking sheet for faster heat transfer to set the crust. This will also catch any juices that bubble over later in the baking process.

If the edges brown before the filling bubbles at the center of the pie, cover it with foil.

pie

Pie Pastry

This recipe combines the great flavor of butter with the superior flaking quality of shortening. Pie pastry made using only shortening is easier to work with, and it will make a wonderfully textured pie crust, but the flavor is not nearly as tasty.

For the flakiest pastry, start with cold ingredients—you don't want those precious blobs of fat to melt until the pie hits the oven. The butter and shortening should be cold, and in the heat of summer I've been known to chill the flour, too. I usually use a pastry blender to cut the fat into the flour, but if you have ice-cold butter and very cold hands, you can even use your fingers—this makes it easy to keep track of the size of the pieces of fat.

Rolling out the dough is easiest on a large sheet of parchment paper or a large wooden pie board. Either should be lightly floured. Use a bench scraper to check that the dough is not sticking, and dust with more flour if necessary.

For baking, I prefer to use thin metal pie plates because they heat up fast in the oven, crisping the pie pastry quickly before the juices from the fruit can make it soggy. Pottery pie plates make a prettier presentation, and glass ones allow you to see if the bottom crust has browned—so use what you like; just watch the baking time, as it may increase. Glass and pottery are heavy, making them slower to heat up and also slower to cool down.

MAKES CRUST FOR ONE 9" STANDARD (OR DEEP-DISH) DOUBLE-CRUST PIE OR FOR TWO 9" TO 10" SINGLE-CRUST PIES.

3 C. all-purpose flour	¾ C. very cold unsalted butter
1 Tbs. sugar	½ C. cold shortening
¾ tsp. salt	8 to 10 Tbs. ice water

In a large bowl, stir together the flour, sugar, and salt until combined. Using the largest holes on a box grater, grate the butter into the flour. Add the cold shortening. Using a pastry blender, cut the fats into the flour until pea-sized clumps begin to form. Drizzle in, while mixing the dough with a large fork, ice water until the dough just starts to come together. Do not overmix. Divide the dough in half and form into two disks. Wrap in plastic and chill before rolling, preferably for at least an hour.

→ **To roll out a single pie or tart crust,** on a lightly floured surface, roll the dough into a circle that's ⅛" to ³⁄₁₆" thick. The circle should be at least 12" for a 9" pie crust, at least 13" for a 10" pie crust, and about 12" for a 9½" tart shell. Gently lay the crust in the pie pan, being very careful not to stretch the dough. Roll the excess dough upon itself to form a cylinder that rests on the edge of the pie pan. Crimp the edge as desired. Prick the bottom and edges of the dough all over with a fork. Chill for 20 minutes, preferably in the freezer.

→ **To blind-bake a single pie crust,** line the chilled pie shell with aluminum foil that overhangs the edge and fill with pie weights or dried beans. Preheat the oven to 425°F. Bake the crust for 20 minutes. Carefully lift out the pie weights with the aluminum foil. Return the crust to the oven and bake 7 to 10 minutes more or until lightly browned on the bottom.

→ **To par-bake a pie or tart crust,** repeat the steps for blind baking, but reduce the baking time after the foil is removed to 5 minutes.

The Myth of Water

Just about every cookbook I own insists that adding too much water to pie dough makes it tough. Truth is, I always use the allotted amount of ice-cold water, and then some, and my pie dough is wonderfully flaky. So what's the deal?

The toughness, as the argument goes, stems from the network of proteins that form when flour and water are mixed. Less water must minimize the formation of protein, then, right? Well, not exactly. Mixing, shaping, and rolling the dough develop the gluten, too—you can feel the dough tighten up as you work it.

Usually the culprit for a tough pie crust is too much mixing, which destroys the pea-sized globs of butter or shortening that make the pastry flaky. Care must be taken not to grind the fat into the flour completely. The action of rolling out the pie pastry develops the gluten, too, and this can contribute to toughness—*but only if you bake the dough right away*. A quick rest in the refrigerator, usually 30 minutes to an hour, relaxes the gluten completely. This step is not to be skipped, or the dough will actually snap back in the oven, losing its shape.

When making pie pastry, I barely work the dough for fear I'll melt all the fat. This means I add more water than most folks as I'm folding and pressing the dough with a rubber spatula to see if it's moist enough to come together. So why is my pie dough so flaky? Think of a quick puff pastry, which has more water than pie dough, has large globs of fat, and gets rolled and folded a lot (for a strong gluten network)—it is tremendously flaky and not tough at all. The key is all in the resting.

Blackberry-Plum Pie with White Almond Streusel

The plums and blackberries of late summer combine to make a wonderful pie. Tart red plums such as Santa Rosa are perfect for this pie. Any kind of blackberry will do, but we all know the ones with the sweetest, most complex flavor are picked by hand or purchased from a local farmers' market. White streusel is an unusual topping for a pie—most streusels are made with brown sugar. But this fluffy, light streusel made with regular sugar lets the fragrance of cardamom and allspice shine through. The toasted almonds add a bit of earthiness. Be sure to only lightly toast the almonds before making the streusel, since they bake again. I like to serve this with vanilla ice cream.

MAKES 8 SERVINGS.

WHITE ALMOND STREUSEL

1 C. all-purpose flour
½ C. chopped lightly toasted almonds
¾ C. sugar

¼ tsp. salt
⅛ tsp. ground allspice
⅛ tsp. ground cardamom
6 Tbs. unsalted butter, melted

FILLING

¾ C. sugar
⅓ C. cornstarch
¼ tsp. salt
1 tsp. ground ginger
¼ tsp. ground allspice

⅛ tsp. freshly grated nutmeg
4 C. pitted, sliced plums (about 12 medium plums)
3 C. blackberries
¼ tsp. almond extract

CRUST

½ recipe Pie Pastry (1 disk; page 183), rolled to fit a standard 9" deep-dish pie pan (into an 11" circle), crimped and chilled

Preheat the oven to 375°F with a baking sheet on the center rack.

For the streusel, in a medium bowl, whisk together the flour, almonds, sugar, salt, and spices. Stir in the melted butter and mix well with your hands. The streusel should be crumbly but form clumps when squeezed. Set aside.

For the filling, in a large bowl, whisk together the sugar, cornstarch, salt, and spices until combined. Add the plums, blackberries, and almond extract; toss to coat evenly.

Scrape the filling into the prepared crust, mounding the filling toward the center. Top with the streusel, breaking apart clumps to get even coverage.

Bake the pie on the preheated baking sheet for 65 to 75 minutes. The filling must be bubbling and thickened near the center of the pie. Cool for 30 minutes on a wire rack. Serve warm.

Blueberry Pie with Lemon Zest & Allspice

I am prone to tossing a few blackberries or nectarines into my blueberry pies, but I live with a blueberry purist who prefers to enjoy the flavor of blueberries at their peak, with little adornment. The pie is flavored with lemon zest and the barest hint of spice—nothing that would take away from the perfect flavor of ripe blueberries. I've seen a lot of blueberry pie recipes that include lemon juice. Though I adore the flavor of lemon with blueberries, I find the addition of lemon juice to be contrary to making a good fruit pie. The juice can't deliver a dose of lemon flavor in a field of packed berries, but it can deliver sourness. Why bother seeking out ripe fruit at its peak of sweet flavor if you plan to make it taste sour? For a nice hit of pure lemon flavor, just use grated lemon zest.

MAKES 8 SERVINGS.

FILLING

¾ C. sugar

⅓ C. cornstarch

2 tsp. grated lemon zest

¼ tsp. salt

⅛ tsp. ground allspice

⅛ tsp. ground cinnamon

8 C. blueberries

2 Tbs. unsalted butter, cut into
   ¾" chunks

CRUST

1 recipe Pie Pastry (2 disks; page 183),
   rolled to fit a 9" standard pie pan
   (into two 11" circles)*

*NOTE: I store the bottom crust fitted into the pie pan with its overhanging edges and the top crust flat on a sheet of parchment paper in the refrigerator until ready to fill the pie.

FINISHING TOUCH

1 Tbs. melted butter for brushing
   top of pie

2 Tbs. sugar for sprinkling top of pie

Preheat the oven to 425°F with a baking sheet on the center rack.

For the filling, in a large bowl, whisk together the sugar, cornstarch, lemon zest, salt, and spices. Add the blueberries and toss to coat evenly.

Scrape the blueberries into the prepared bottom crust, mounding the filling toward the center. Sprinkle the chunks of butter over the filling. Cut vents in the top crust and lay over the blueberries. Roll the overhanging bottom and top crust edges together into a cylinder that rests on the edge of the pie pan. Crimp the edge as desired.

For the finishing touch, brush the top of the pie with the melted butter and sprinkle with the sugar. Chill the pie, preferably in the freezer, for at least 15 minutes.

Bake the pie on the preheated baking sheet for 15 minutes. Reduce the heat to 375°F and bake for 50 to 55 minutes or until the filling bubbling out the center vents is thickened. Cool for 30 minutes on a wire rack.

My mother was crazy about peach pie. I remember her taking us to the orchard in summer to pick peaches, and then returning home to watch her spend the better part of a day making pies. Since she was a convenience-food cook, and not a good one at that, I refer to this annual event as her summer "pie madness." Once you've made a few homemade pies, you'll understand what came over her—the pastry is crisp, the filling is not overly sweet, and the fruit is incredibly fragrant. Though today my pie madness includes every fruit in season from May to October, this is the pie that started it all.

You'll notice I take a shortcut and don't peel the peaches. If you are a purist, like my mother and grandmother, here's how to peel them: First, bring a pan of water to a boil. Lightly cut a small X at the bottom of the peach (opposite the stem), then dip the peaches in the simmering water for 30 seconds or so to loosen the skins. Immerse the peaches in a bowl of ice-cold water to stop the cooking, then peel them one at a time. The fuzzy skin will slip right off.

MAKES 8 SERVINGS.

FILLING

⅔ C. sugar

⅓ C. cornstarch

1 tsp. ground ginger

¼ tsp. ground cinnamon

¼ tsp. freshly grated nutmeg

¼ tsp. salt

8 C. unpeeled, pitted, and sliced ripe
    peaches (about 8 peaches)

CRUST

1 recipe Pie Pastry (2 disks; page 183),
    rolled to fit a 9" standard pie pan
    (into two 11" circles)

FINISHING TOUCH

1 Tbs. melted butter for brushing top
    of pie

2 Tbs. sugar for sprinkling top of pie

Preheat the oven to 425°F with a baking sheet on the center rack.

For the filling, in a large bowl, whisk together the sugar, cornstarch, spices, and salt. Add the peaches and toss to coat evenly.

Scrape the filling into the prepared bottom crust, mounding the filling toward the center. Cut vents in the top crust and lay over the peaches. Roll the overhanging bottom and top crust edges together into a cylinder that rests on the edge of the pie pan. Crimp the edge as desired.

For the finishing touch, brush the top of the pie with the melted butter and sprinkle with the sugar. Chill the pie, preferably in the freezer, for at least 15 minutes.

Bake the pie on the preheated baking sheet for 60 to 70 minutes or until the filling bubbling out the center vents is thickened. Cool for 30 minutes on a wire rack.

Apple Pie with Cheddar Streusel

I love any apple pie, so it's hard to choose just one for this book. My personal favorite, though, is an apple pie made with crisp, tart apples and topped with a streusel. Not just any streusel, but one made with sharp cheddar cheese. In New England, apple pie is often served with a slice of cheddar, but I prefer to use the tangy flavor of good cheddar in a crunchy-chewy streusel. It's heavenly.

MAKES 8 SERVINGS.

CHEDDAR STREUSEL

1 C. all-purpose flour
1 C. shredded sharp cheddar cheese
½ C. sugar
⅛ tsp. salt
¼ cup unsalted butter, melted

FILLING

⅓ C. sugar
¼ C. all-purpose flour
1 tsp. grated lemon zest
1 tsp. ground cinnamon
⅛ tsp. ground cloves
⅛ tsp. freshly grated nutmeg
¼ tsp. salt
8 cups peeled, cored, and sliced tart
　　baking apples (3 lbs. or about 8
　　Granny Smith apples)
2 Tbs. lemon juice

CRUST

½ recipe Pie Pastry (1 disk; page 183),
　　rolled to fit a 9" deep-dish pie pan
　　(into a 13" circle), crimped and
　　chilled

Preheat the oven to 375°F with a baking sheet on the center rack.

For the streusel, in a medium bowl, whisk together the flour, cheese, sugar, and salt. Stir in the melted butter and mix well with your hands. The streusel should be crumbly but form clumps when squeezed. Set aside.

For the filling, in a large bowl, whisk together the sugar, flour, lemon zest, spices, and salt. Add the apples and lemon juice and toss to coat evenly.

Scrape the apples into the prepared crust, mounding the filling toward the center. Top with the streusel, breaking apart clumps to get even coverage.

Bake the pie on the preheated baking sheet for 60 to 70 minutes. The filling must be bubbling and thickened near the center of the pie. Cool for 30 minutes on a wire rack. Serve warm.

Cherry-Berry Pie

In the heart of summer, I'll admit that my pie baking is improvisational—meaning that whatever fruit I see in the refrigerator goes into the pie. That's how I happened upon the wonderful combination of cherries with summer berries like raspberries and blueberries. I think I've had as many as five varieties of berries in the pie at once, and it always tastes wonderful. I especially adore cherries, but the season for the true pie cherry (also known as sour or tart cherries) is short, just about two weeks where I live. If you are fortunate to be able to buy them fresh, tart, bright red pie cherries make the best pies ever. The sweeter cherries don't have the same perky flavor, but they work great in combination with other tart berries.

MAKES 8 SERVINGS.

FILLING

1¼ C. sugar

⅓ C. cornstarch

¼ tsp. salt

¼ tsp. ground allspice

¼ tsp. ground cinnamon

4 C. sour cherries or sweet cherries, pitted

2 C. blackberries or raspberries

2 C. blueberries

¼ tsp. almond extract

CRUST

1 recipe Pie Pastry (2 disks; page 183–184), rolled to fit a 9" standard pie pan (into two 11" circles)

FINISHING TOUCH

1 Tbs. melted butter for brushing top of pie

2 Tbs. sugar for sprinkling top of pie

Preheat the oven to 375°F with a baking sheet on the center rack.

For the filling, in a large bowl, whisk together the sugar, cornstarch, salt, and spices until combined. Add the cherries, berries, and almond extract and toss to coat evenly.

Scrape the filling into the prepared bottom crust, mounding the filling toward the center. Cut vents in the top crust (you can even use a decorative cookie cutter) and lay over the berries. Roll the overhanging bottom and top crust edges together into a cylinder that rests on the edge of the pie pan. Crimp the edge as desired.

For the finishing touch, brush the top of the pie with the melted butter and sprinkle with the sugar. Chill the pie, preferably in the freezer, for at least 15 minutes.

Bake the pie on the preheated baking sheet for 1 hour and 20 minutes to 1½ hours or until the filling bubbling out the center vents is thickened. Cool for 30 minutes on a wire rack.

I am a huge fan of strawberry pie, so although rhubarb and raspberries make an appearance in this pie, it's really all about showing off the flavor of the strawberries. You'll notice that the majority of the strawberries are stirred into the fruit mixture at the end of the cooking time. This preserves the flavor, color, and texture of the strawberries, filling every bite of pie with a burst of fresh berry flavor. These pie slices will be a bit loose, not super-firm like diner pie, as the undercooked berries continue to release water. It is utterly delicious, but if you prefer the fruit to set into a rigid gel, cook all the berries together and add the starch mixture at the very end. The pie filling does not entirely fill the shell, leaving plenty of room to pile on the whipped cream.

MAKES 8 SERVINGS.

FILLING

1 C. chopped rhubarb (1 large stalk)	½ tsp. ground ginger
1 C. raspberries or loganberries	⅛ tsp. ground allspice
1 C. strawberries, halved, plus 2 C. quartered strawberries	¼ C. cornstarch
	¼ C. water
¾ C. sugar	

CRUST

One blind-baked 9" Pie Pastry crust (page 183–184)

TOPPING

1¼ C. heavy whipping cream	2 Tbs. powdered sugar

For the filling, in a medium saucepan over medium-high heat, combine the rhubarb, raspberries or loganberries, and the halved strawberries with the sugar, ginger, and allspice. Heat until very hot but not boiling. Dissolve the cornstarch in the water and add to the berry mixture. Cook, stirring constantly, for 1 minute. Stir in the quartered strawberries and cook for 1 minute. Pour into the prepared baked shell. Chill until completely set, about 3 hours.

For the topping, in a chilled bowl with a chilled whisk, beat the heavy cream with the sugar until stiff peaks form. Spread the whipped cream over the top of the cold pie.

Pumpkin Pie with Coconut Milk & Rum

Shake up your Thanksgiving this year by adding a Caribbean twist to pumpkin pie. Coconut milk, rum, and an unusual spice mixture breathe new life into this traditional favorite. Because a soggy crust is my pet peeve, I par-bake the pie shell first to give it a head start on crispness before the filling is added. I also heat up the milk before whisking the ingredients together. A warm batter helps the custard cook faster in the oven, further ensuring that you'll have a crisp crust for at least the first 24 hours.

MAKES 8 SERVINGS.

FILLING

1¼ C. unsweetened coconut milk
1 (15-oz.) can pumpkin puree
⅔ C. packed dark brown sugar
1 tsp. ground ginger
½ tsp. ground cardamom
¼ tsp. ground allspice

¼ tsp. ground cinnamon
⅛ tsp. freshly grated nutmeg
¼ tsp. salt
4 large eggs
2 Tbs. dark rum

CRUST

One par-baked 9" Pie Pastry crust (page 183)

Preheat the oven to 425°F with a baking sheet on the center rack.

In a medium saucepan, bring the coconut milk to a boil. Turn off the heat. Whisk in the pumpkin puree, brown sugar, spices, and salt until smooth. One at a time, add the eggs, whisking constantly. Stir in the rum.

Pour the filling into the prepared baked shell. Bake the pie on the pre-heated baking sheet for 10 minutes, and then reduce the oven temperature to 350°F. Bake for another 30 to 35 minutes, until the center of the pie no longer wobbles when the pan is moved.

Let the pie cool completely on a wire rack before serving. Serve with lightly sweetened whipped cream.

tarts

Fresh Berry Tart

I fell in love with pastry early in life, and from my first trip to the local bakery I was smitten with fresh berry tarts. Good ones are hard to find, so now I make them myself. The texture and flavor contrasts offered by the combination of a crunchy, buttery crust filled with vanilla cream and topped with ripe berries is really hard to beat. As simple as this dessert is, it makes a beautiful presentation. If you plan to make this dessert a day ahead, I do recommend coating the berries with the glaze—it protects the custard and keeps any cut edges on the fruit from drying out. Another old pastry-chef trick is to place a very thin layer of sponge cake lightly brushed with a liqueur under the pastry cream to absorb moisture and keep the crust crisp longer.

MAKES 8 SERVINGS.

SWEET DOUGH CRUST

1½ C. all-purpose flour
2 Tbs. sugar
½ tsp. salt

½ C. very cold unsalted butter
1 large egg yolk
2 Tbs. heavy whipping cream

FILLING

1⅔ C. Bourbon Vanilla Pastry Cream
(page 225)

3 C. any combination of fresh
raspberries, blueberries, and/or
halved strawberries

GLAZE (OPTIONAL)

¼ C. jelly or seedless preserves, such
as red currant or raspberry
2 Tbs. water

1 Tbs. framboise or other berry
liqueur

For the Sweet Dough Crust, in a medium bowl, stir together the flour, sugar, and salt. Using the largest holes on a box grater, grate the butter into the flour. Using a pastry blender, cut the butter into the flour until pea-sized clumps begin to form. Mix together the egg yolk and the cream. Drizzle in enough of the egg mixture, while mixing the dough with a large fork, until the dough just starts to come together. Do not overmix. Form the dough into a disk and wrap in plastic. Chill before rolling, preferably for at least an hour.

On a lightly floured surface, roll the dough into an 11" circle, ⅛" to ³⁄₁₆" thick. Gently lay the crust into a 9½" removable-bottom tart pan, being very careful not to stretch the dough. Roll the excess dough upon itself to form a cylinder that rests on the edge of the pan. Crimp the edge as desired. (Or, for the easiest crust, fold excess dough over edge of the tart pan and, using the flat of a knife, trim off the excess dough with gentle pressure.) Prick the bottom and the edges of dough all over with a fork. Chill for 20 minutes, preferably in the freezer. Line the tart shell with aluminum foil that overhangs the edge and fill with pie weights or dried beans.

Preheat the oven to 375°F. Bake the crust for 20 minutes. Carefully lift out the pie weights with the aluminum foil. Return the crust to the oven and bake 7 to 10 minutes more or until lightly browned on the bottom. Cool completely on a wire rack.

Spoon the Pastry Cream into the cooled tart shell, leveling with an off-set spatula. Top with fresh berries, arranging in an attractive pattern, if desired, or just heaping them on for a more rustic, yet still charming, effect.

For the glaze, if desired, in a small saucepan combine the jelly, water, and liqueur over medium-low heat. Heat, stirring occasionally, until the jelly is completely melted and fluid. Coat the fruit and any exposed pastry cream with the mixture using a pastry brush and a gentle dabbing motion, letting the glaze flow over the fruit rather than brushing on vigorously. Refrigerate until ready to serve.

Hazelnut-Blackberry Meringue Tart

Fluffy sweet meringue, tart blackberries, and toasted hazelnuts give this tart layers of delightfully contrasting textures and flavors. Almonds, pecans, walnuts, peanuts, and macadamia nuts all work well in this versatile crust that I use as base for all kinds of tarts and pies. Though blackberries and hazelnuts are regional favorites here in the Pacific Northwest, there is definitely an old-world quality about this dessert. The meringue is simple and foolproof: Adding a bit of thickened cornstarch and water to the egg whites stabilizes the meringue and prevents it from "weeping" when cooled.

MAKES 8 SERVINGS.

GRAHAM-NUT CRUST

⅓ C. whole hazelnuts	3 Tbs. sugar
1 pkg. (one-third of a 14-oz. box, 9 cracker rectangles) graham crackers, finely crushed (1 C.)	⅛ tsp. salt
	4 Tbs. unsalted butter, melted

FILLING

1⅔ C. blackberries	¼ tsp. ground allspice
1⅔ C. blueberries	1½ tsp. cornstarch
½ C. sugar	1 Tbs. water

MERINGUE

¼ C. water	2 large egg whites, at room
¼ C. sugar	temperature
2 tsp. cornstarch	⅛ tsp. salt

For the Graham-Nut Crust, preheat the oven to 350°F. Using a rotary grater, grind the hazelnuts finely. Or, place the nuts (this works great for the graham crackers, too) in a heavy-duty plastic food-storage bag and crush them with a rolling pin. Another option is to chop the nuts very finely on a cutting board with a big chef's knife or cleaver. Slightly different textures are achieved with each technique, but they are all nice—and low-tech.

In a medium bowl, stir together the graham cracker crumbs, hazelnuts, sugar, and salt. Drizzle in the butter and stir until well combined. Press the mixture into the bottom and up the sides of a 9½"-round tart pan with a removable bottom. Bake for 10 minutes or until the crust is set. Cool completely on a wire rack.

For the filling, in a medium saucepan over medium-high heat, combine the blackberries, blueberries, sugar, and allspice. Bring to a boil and continue cooking, stirring occasionally, until thickened, 6 to 8 minutes. Dissolve the cornstarch in the water and add to the berry mixture. Cook, stirring constantly, until the mixture is very thick, at least 1 minute. Spread the warm berry filling over the prepared crust and keep warm.

Increase the oven temperature to 425°F. For the meringue, in a small saucepan, stir together the water, sugar, and cornstarch until dissolved. Place over medium heat and cook, stirring constantly, until thickened, about 2 minutes. Cool to warm and add the egg whites and salt. Using a balloon whisk, beat the mixture until stiff peaks form, about 2 minutes.

Spread the meringue over the filling using an offset spatula, making sure it goes all the way to the edge and pressing lightly to adhere. Place the tart on a baking sheet to insulate the crust and bake for 8 to 9 minutes or until the meringue is browned on the peaks. Serve warm or cold.

Plum Frangipane Tarts

I've always loved the almond filling called frangipane that's a staple in Euro-pean pastries. Turns out it's a cinch to make, and if you start with frozen puff pastry, you can turn out an elegant French-style pastry in no time at all. The flavor of fresh red plums with the almond filling is wonderful, but any seasonal tart fruit will do the trick. Apricots, blackberries, sour cherries, or cranberries are equally tasty with the almond paste. Frangipane is quite versatile: You can spread it over a rolled galette dough (see page 50) before piling on the fruit, or make a fruit tart with it by spreading it over par-baked Sweet Dough Crust (see page 201) and baking it with sliced plums and apricots on top.

MAKES 8 SERVINGS.

½ C. toasted sliced almonds
3 Tbs. unsalted butter, at room
  temperature
¼ C. sugar
⅛ tsp. salt
2 large egg yolks, divided
¼ tsp. vanilla extract
⅛ tsp. almond extract

1 Tbs. all-purpose flour
1 sheet frozen puff pastry (half of a
  17.3-oz. box), thawed
1 Tbs. water
4 small tart plums, such as Santa
  Rosa, halved and pitted
Sugar for sprinkling

For the frangipane, grind the almonds finely in a rotary grater; set aside. In a medium bowl, beat together the butter, sugar, and salt until smooth and creamy, about 1 minute. Beat in one of the egg yolks and the extracts. Beat in the flour and the ground almonds; set aside.

Preheat the oven to 400°F. Line a baking sheet with parchment paper. On a lightly floured surface, unfold the piece of puff pastry and cut into three strips following the seams that are apparent when the pastry is unfolded. Cut one of these smaller rectangles into five strips lengthwise, each about ⅜" wide. Place the two larger puff pastry rectangles on the baking sheet at least 3" apart. Brush the edges of each rectangle with some water using a pastry brush. Lay four of the skinny strips of pastry along the long edges of the two big rectangles. Cut the remaining skinny strip into 4 pieces; lay across the short ends of the rectangles to complete the border. Whisk the remaining egg yolk with the 1 tablespoon water. Brush over the border around each rectangle. Using a small, sharp knife, score the border very lightly in a decorative pattern. Chill for 15 minutes.

Divide the frangipane evenly among the two shells, using an offset spatula to spread the filling evenly right up to the border.

Using a small, sharp knife, cut each plum half into a fan, leaving the slices attached at one end. Fan four of the plum halves over the frangipane in each tart. Sprinkle with sugar. Bake for 25 to 27 minutes or until the pastry is golden and puffed, the plums are softened and lightly caramelized, and the frangipane is set but still moist. Cool on the pan for 5 minutes and then transfer to a wire rack to cool for another 5 to 10 minutes. Serve warm.

Cranberry, Pear, & Walnut Tart

Tart cranberries contrast nicely with sweet, ripe pears in this festive autumn tart. Fragrant ground cardamom and spicy crystallized ginger give a flavor boost to the usual suspects, cinnamon and allspice. Topped with a walnut streusel, this colorful tart is a wonderful finish to holiday meals. The tart tastes best when served just barely warm, with a scoop of vanilla ice cream on the side.

MAKES 10 SERVINGS.

CRANBERRY-PEAR FILLING

⅔ C. sugar

3 Tbs. finely minced crystallized ginger

2 tsp. all-purpose flour

½ tsp. ground cardamom

¼ tsp. ground cinnamon

⅛ tsp. ground allspice

⅛ tsp. salt

3 large ripe pears, peeled, quartered lengthwise, cored, and cut crosswise into ¼"-thick slices

2 cups fresh cranberries, coarsely chopped

1 Tbs. brandy

CRUST

1 recipe Sweet Dough Crust (page 201), rolled and par-baked (5 minutes less time than in Sweet Dough Crust instructions) in a 9½" removable-bottom tart pan.

WALNUT STREUSEL

⅓ C. plus 1 Tbs. all-purpose flour

¼ C. packed light brown sugar

¼ C. chopped walnuts

⅛ tsp. salt

2 Tbs. unsalted butter, melted

¼ tsp. vanilla extract

Preheat the oven to 350°F. For the filling, in a medium bowl, whisk together the sugar, ginger, flour, spices, and salt. Add the pears, cranberries, and brandy and toss to coat. Spoon the filling into the par-baked tart shell, leveling and packing down slightly with the back of a spoon.

For the streusel, in a small bowl, mix the flour, brown sugar, walnuts, and salt. Add the melted butter and vanilla. Mix until the mixture clumps together when squeezed.

Sprinkle the streusel over the filling, breaking it into smaller pieces if necessary. Bake until the fruit is tender when pierced with a fork and the streusel is golden, 45 to 50 minutes. If the tart begins to get overly brown at the edges, cover the edges with foil. Cool on a wire rack until just warm.

other
fruity
desserts

Nectarine, Raspberry, & Rhubarb Crisp

This versatile recipe is really great throughout the year—the combination of nectarine, raspberry, and rhubarb takes good advantage of what is available in midsummer, but give it a try in the fall with apples and cranberries in the variation given below. The streusel is great to make in big batches and freeze. Use it directly from the freezer to top whatever great fruit you bring back from the market or the farm.

SERVES 6.

4 C. sliced nectarines (about 3 large)
3 C. raspberries
2 cups ½" pieces rhubarb (about
    2 small stalks)
1 C. sugar
2 Tbs. cornstarch
¼ tsp. ground allspice

¼ tsp. ground cardamom
1 C. all-purpose flour
⅓ C. packed light brown sugar
⅓ C. old-fashioned rolled oats
¼ tsp. salt
¼ C. unsalted butter, melted

Preheat the oven to 375°F. Butter a 9"-square baking dish. Combine the nectarines, raspberries, rhubarb, sugar, cornstarch, allspice, and cardamom in the baking dish and mix well.

In a small bowl, combine the flour, brown sugar, oats, and salt. Stir in the melted butter. Mix until the mixture clumps together when squeezed. Sprinkle the oat mixture over the fruit. Bake for 40 minutes or until the fruit mixture is bubbly and thickened near the center of the dish and the streusel is golden.

→ **APPLE-CRANBERRY CRISP:** Substitute 5 cups chopped tart baking apples (4 to 5 apples) and one 12-ounce package fresh or frozen cranberries for the nectarines, raspberries, and rhubarb. Substitute cinnamon for the allspice and a pinch of cloves for the cardamom.

Drop-Biscuit Fruit Cobbler

Fruit cobbler is such a regular at my house that I've stopped thinking of it as specific to certain fruit: I just use whatever I have on hand. Here I feature peaches and blueberries, but any combination of fruit will work, so long as you have about 8 cups total. Peaches and blueberries are pretty sweet, so I've kept the amount of sugar to a minimum. If you use tart fruit, like blackberries or rhubarb, you'll need more sugar.

To ensure a thoroughly cooked topping, I always bake the fruit by itself until very hot before I top it with the batter. Either fresh or thawed frozen fruit is fine for this cobbler, but be sure to measure the frozen fruit right out of the freezer—it will collapse as it thaws. If you start with fruit that is very cold, you'll need to increase the baking times (before and after applying the biscuit topping) by at least 5 minutes. Serve this with ice cream.

MAKES 8 SERVINGS.

FRUIT FILLING

5 C. sliced peaches (about 5)	⅛ tsp. salt
3 C. blueberries	⅛ tsp. ground cinnamon
⅓ C. sugar	⅛ tsp. freshly grated nutmeg
2 Tbs. cornstarch	

DROP-BISCUIT TOPPING

1 C. all-purpose flour	¼ C. cold unsalted butter
2 Tbs. plus 1½ tsp. sugar	½ C. milk
1¼ tsp. baking powder	¼ tsp. vanilla extract
¼ tsp. salt	Sugar for sprinkling

Preheat the oven to 350°F. Butter a 9"-square or -round baking dish. Combine the peaches, blueberries, sugar, cornstarch, salt, cinnamon, and nutmeg in the baking dish and mix well. Bake for 20 minutes.

Meanwhile, prepare the topping. In a large bowl, whisk together the flour, sugar, baking powder, and salt. Using the largest holes on a box grater, grate the butter into the flour mixture. Using a pastry blender, cut in the butter until the largest clumps are pea-sized. Using a large fork, gradually mix in the milk and vanilla until the dough just comes together.

After the fruit has baked for the initial 20 minutes, remove the pan from the oven and dollop the topping over the hot fruit. Sprinkle the topping with sugar and return to the oven. Bake for 25 to 30 minutes more or until the fruit mixture is bubbling and thickened near the center and the biscuits are golden. Serve warm.

Pear Tarte Tatin with Lemon and Anise

This recipe was inspired by a luscious dessert I had at a local Portland restaurant. Light, crisp, and not at all filling, it was the perfect way to end a meal. I can't say that pears have ever been my favorite fruit, but the perky lemon zest and light scent of crushed anise really makes the pears shine. Be sure to use pears that are just beginning to ripen—overripe pears will disintegrate into mush too quickly. To check for ripeness, press the neck of the pear near the stem. If it is slightly soft, the pear is ripe. If it's hard, the pear is not ready to be used.

MAKES 6 SERVINGS.

1 sheet prepared frozen puff pastry (half of a 17.3-oz. box), thawed
3 medium pears, peeled, cored, and each cut lengthwise into 8 pieces
1 Tbs. freshly squeezed lemon juice
¼ C. unsalted butter
¼ of 1 vanilla bean
1 tsp. grated lemon zest
1 tsp. anise seed, crushed with the flat side of a heavy knife
¼ C. sugar

Preheat the oven to 400°F. On a lightly floured surface, roll the sheet of puff pastry into an 11" square. Trim the square into a 10½"-diameter circle, discarding the scrap or saving for another use. Place the pastry circle in the refrigerator on a baking sheet until needed.

In a large bowl, toss the pear slices with the lemon juice. Melt the butter in a 9" heavy ovenproof skillet over medium heat. Cut the vanilla bean in half lengthwise and scrape out the seeds. Add the vanilla bean seeds, the lemon zest, and the anise seeds to the skillet and cook for 1 minute. Remove from the heat and add the pear slices to the skillet, arranging them in a fan around the outer edge and fitting in as many as possible. Fill in the center of the skillet with remaining pear slices. Sprinkle with the sugar.

Drape the puff pastry circle over the pears, tucking the pastry in between the skillet and the fruit. Bake for 25 to 30 minutes or until the pastry is puffed and deeply golden. Cool in the pan on a wire rack for 3 minutes. Place a serving plate over the skillet and carefully invert the skillet to unmold the Tarte Tatin onto the plate. Serve immediately.

Sour Cherry Strudel

This delectable, flaky pastry will have you hooked on strudel. I've packed it about as full as possible with a chunky tart-cherry filling, so each bite explodes with both shards of light pastry and delectable fruit. Thanks to frozen phyllo sheets—the perfect stand-in for homemade strudel dough—the recipe is fast and easy. I like to have a box of phyllo on hand in the freezer to be ready whenever a craving for strudel hits. You can use any fruit for the filling, so long as you precook it on the stove top, as I did here, to thicken the juices and prevent the strudel from getting soggy. The filling for the Apple Turnovers (page 217) also makes a great strudel.

MAKES 6 SERVINGS.

3½ C. fresh or thawed frozen sour cherries, pitted, with their juices (1 lb.)

½ C. sugar

1 Tbs. plus 2 tsp. cornstarch

2 Tbs. brandy, kirsch, or amaretto

⅛ tsp. almond extract

¼ tsp. salt

6 Tbs. unsalted butter, melted

3 Tbs. graham cracker crumbs

3 Tbs. panko (Japanese-style bread crumbs)

2 Tbs. toasted whole almonds, finely ground in a rotary grater or finely chopped

½ of a 1-lb. box frozen phyllo dough, thawed*

Powdered sugar for dusting

*NOTE: Most phyllo dough comes in a 1-pound box, divided into two 8-ounce individually wrapped packets, each containing 20 sheets of phyllo. For this recipe, I thaw one of those 8-ounce packets and leave the other one frozen. Of those thawed 20 sheets, I will use 7 for this strudel. Phyllo sheets are quite fragile and will occasionally will rip or stick together. Thawing the 20 sheets ensures you will have plenty for the strudel. The remaining sheets should keep, assuming you have handled them with care as noted below, rerolled and wrapped tightly in plastic, in the refrigerator for up to 10 days. You should have enough left for another strudel or some baklava.

In a medium saucepan over medium-high heat, combine the cherries with their liquid and the sugar. Dissolve the cornstarch in the chosen liquor and add to the pan. Cook, stirring constantly, until the mixture just boils and thickens, 3 to 4 minutes. Remove from the heat and stir in the almond extract. Cool completely. Stir the salt into the melted butter and set aside.

Preheat the oven to 375°F. In a small bowl, combine the graham cracker crumbs, panko crumbs, and almonds; set aside. Unroll the sheets of phyllo to one side of the work surface, covering them first, with a sheet of plastic wrap then with damp paper towels to keep the phyllo from drying out. Place a sheet of parchment paper on the work surface. Place one sheet of phyllo on the parchment, covering the remaining sheets again. Brush the sheet of phyllo with some of the butter, starting at the outer edges, which tend to dry out first, and then brushing to the center. Sprinkle with 1 tablespoon of the crumb mixture. Repeat the process layering five more sheets of phyllo, brushing each sheet with the melted butter and sprinkling with the 1 tablespoon crumbs. Add the seventh and final sheet of phyllo, brushing with butter and sprinkling with the remaining 2 tablespoons crumbs.

Spoon the filling along the long side of the phyllo stack, leaving a ½" border on both the long and short edges. Fold the ½" short edges and the long border edge over the filling and roll up, jelly-roll style, using the parchment paper to help guide the roll. Finish with the seam on the bottom, rolling the entire strudel if necessary to make sure the seam side is down. Lift the strudel with the parchment onto a large baking sheet. Brush with the remaining melted butter. Bake for 24 to 25 minutes or until the phyllo is deep golden brown. Cool for 15 minutes on the baking sheet. Dust with powdered sugar. Using a serrated knife, cut the strudel into slices.

Apple Turnovers

If you keep a package of frozen puff pastry sheets on hand, you can throw a lovely treat together at a moment's notice. The apple filling recipe is from ex–pastry chef Lisa Bell, and it's my all-time favorite chunky apple-sauce, flavored with a real vanilla bean and just lightly spiced. I make it in large batches and freeze it for pies, tarts, galettes, and turnovers, and even for just eating plain. Be sure not to cook the apples too long—they will cook a second time in the turnovers, so you'll want to leave them a bit firm.

MAKES 8 LARGE TURNOVERS.

5 C. chopped apples (about 5 apples, peeled, cored, and cut into 1½" pieces)

½ C. sugar

3 Tbs. water

½ of 1 vanilla bean (split lengthwise), seeds scraped out and pod reserved

1 tsp. grated lemon zest

¼ tsp. ground cinnamon

4 whole cloves

2 sheets (one 17.3-oz. box) frozen puff pastry, thawed

GLAZE

1 egg yolk beaten with 1 Tbs. water   Sugar for sprinkling

In a large skillet over medium-high heat, combine the apples, sugar, water, vanilla bean seeds and pod, lemon zest, cinnamon, and cloves. Cook, stirring occasionally, until the apples just soften but still retain their shape and most of the liquid has evaporated. Cool completely. Remove the vanilla bean pod and the cloves and discard.

Preheat the oven to 400°F. Line two baking sheets with parchment paper. On a lightly floured surface, roll one sheet of the puff pastry into a 12" square. Cut this square into four 6" squares. Repeat with the remaining sheet of puff pastry. Place ⅓ cup apple filling just off center in one square. Brush the edges of the square with water. Fold the puff pastry over the filling to form a triangle. Using the tines of a fork, lightly press around the edges of the turnover to seal. Repeat with the remaining filling and the remaining puff pastry squares. Place the turnovers on the baking sheets, spacing at least 2" apart. Brush the tops of the turnovers with the egg glaze and sprinkle with sugar. Using a small, sharp knife, cut a steam vent in the top of each turnover. Bake for 24 to 25 minutes or until puffed and very well browned. Cool the turnovers on wire rack. Serve warm or cold.

Raspberry–Lemon Cream Trifle

Trifles are a great way to serve dessert because they require absolutely no decorating skills whatsoever, and they taste creamy, light, and fresh. They're also perfect make-ahead desserts, as they are best prepared a few hours before serving. It's funny—I've noticed that guests take tiny portions of fancy layer cakes but large helpings of trifle. It's all the same, really, but I think the mousse-like airy filling and berries make trifles seem like, well, merely a trifle.

MAKES 16 SERVINGS.

1 recipe Golden Yellow Cake Layers (page 174)
1 C. heavy whipping cream

1 recipe Lemon Curd (page 227)
3 C. fresh raspberries or blueberries

With a serrated knife, cut the cake layers into ¾" cubes. Using a chilled metal bowl and balloon whisk, whip the heavy cream until stiff peaks form. Fold one-quarter of the whipped cream into the lemon curd to lighten it, and then fold in rest of the whipped cream with a rubber spatula. Place about one-third of the cake cubes in the bottom of a trifle bowl. Dollop with about one-third of the lemon cream. Sprinkle with 1 cup of the berries. Repeat twice more, finishing with the berries. Chill until ready to serve. Let stand for 15 minutes at room temperature before serving.

08.

CREAMY DESSERTS

the desserts in this chapter range from simple mousses to layered pies, but they are all unified by the flavor and texture of cream. Most of them are dinner-party fare, elegant enough to wow guests, but that does not necessarily mean complex. The individual panna cottas and pots de crème take only minutes to prepare.

Because many of these desserts depend on a light, airy texture for their quality, this is the chapter to review the master technique of folding. Aggressive mixing will reduce the finished volume of your dessert, so it pays to get it right. Using a silicone spatula, cut down through the batter at the center of the bowl, then run the spatula under the batter while pulling it toward you. When you get to the edge of the bowl, scoop the batter up and fold it over by turning the spatula. If you fold the batter with the spatula in your right hand, you can use your left hand to rotate the bowl. When folding whipped cream into mousse, or egg whites into a denser batter, it's easiest to take a small portion of your cream or whites and gently whisk them into the mixture—this lightens the mixture and makes it easier to quickly and efficiently fold in the remaining whipped cream or whites.

Bourbon Vanilla Pastry Cream (or Plain Old Pudding)

Vanilla pudding sounds plain to some, but I can assure you there's nothing plain about this wonderfully creamy custard. I use it to fill cakes like Boston Cream Pie (page 170), and I also like to lighten it with whipped cream and then layer it with cubed cake, fresh berries, and liqueur for a lovely summer trifle. Spread it over a prebaked puff pastry shell and you can assemble a gorgeous fruit tart. Thicken it more (increase the cornstarch to ⅓ cup) and the pudding becomes pastry cream, perfect for layering those puff pastry sheets into a berry Napoleon. You can omit the brandy if you like, but the vanilla bean is essential to this custard. I favor vanilla beans from Madagascar and other islands in the Indian Ocean, which are known as Bourbon vanilla. Mexican vanilla beans also have a lovely flavor.

MAKES 2¾ CUPS.

1 vanilla bean, split in half lengthwise
1½ C. milk
1 C. heavy whipping cream
4 large egg yolks
½ C. sugar

⅓ C. cornstarch (reduce to ¼ C. for pudding)
¼ tsp. salt
1 Tbs. Cognac or bourbon
2 Tbs. unsalted butter

On a flat surface, using a small knife, scrape the seeds out of each vanilla bean half. In a medium saucepan, combine the milk, heavy whipping cream, vanilla seeds, and vanilla bean pods. Bring to a simmer over medium heat. Remove from the heat and let stand for 10 minutes.

In a medium bowl, whisk together the egg yolks, sugar, cornstarch, and salt until smooth. Return the saucepan with the vanilla mixture to high heat; bring to a boil. Slowly pour half of the hot milk mixture into the yolk mixture, whisking constantly. Return the egg mixture to the pan; reduce the heat to medium-low. Cook, stirring constantly, until the mixture thickens and bubbles, 2 to 3 minutes. Remove from the heat and stir in the Cognac or bourbon and the butter. Strain the filling through a fine-mesh sieve into a container. Cover the surface directly with plastic wrap and chill for 3 hours.

White Chocolate Whipped Cream

White chocolate whipped cream is really a form of whipped ganache—just a bit heartier than whipped cream. There is more cream than chocolate, making a light filling, frosting, or accompaniment for any dessert. You can add a bit more chocolate if you want a denser whipped filling, but more white chocolate will make it sweeter. Most white chocolate includes a bit of vanilla, but you may want to add a bit more, or perhaps a favorite liqueur or citrus zest for flavor. Any ganache that is to be whipped needs to rest and cool for at least 8 hours or it will not whip properly. You will need to plan ahead when making white chocolate whipped cream, but it's a wonderfully versatile component and can be used for everything from topping dark chocolate cupcakes to serving with berries and shortcake. You can even fold in lemon curd and turn it into a mousse. White chocolate whipped cream is only as good as the chocolate you use, so be sure to taste before you start. I've listed my brand preferences below.

MAKES ABOUT 2¼ CUPS.

1 C. heavy whipping cream

1 (3.5-oz.) bar Lindt or Rainforest white chocolate, coarsely chopped

In a small saucepan, bring the cream to a boil over medium-high heat. Remove the pan from the heat and add the chocolate. Let stand for 1 minute. Whisk until the chocolate is melted and the mixture is smooth. Transfer to a medium bowl, cover the surface directly with plastic wrap, and refrigerate overnight or for at least 8 hours. Whip with a whisk until just past the soft-peak stage or until the mixture is firm enough to hold its shape and be spreadable. Do not overbeat as it will make the cream hard and dry.

Lemon Curd

This lemon curd is tart, making it perfect for serving with a slice of chiffon cake or a cream scone. You can use it to make a French *tarte au citron*: Simply spread the curd in a prebaked Sweet Dough Crust (page 201) and bake until set. It's also wonderful as a filling in cakes, such as the Lemon Coconut Cloud Cake (page 172). Try spreading a thin layer of blackberry preserves on a yellow cake layer, then topping it with lemon curd—serve the cake with fresh blueberries and blackberries. My favorite way to enjoy lemon curd is to make a light mousse out of it by folding in whipped cream—this is how the filling for the Raspberry–Lemon Cream Trifle (page 219) is made.

MAKES 1¾ CUPS.

¾ C. sugar	2 tsp. grated lemon zest
⅔ C. lemon juice	2 large eggs
6 Tbs. unsalted butter	4 large egg yolks

In a medium saucepan, whisk together the sugar, lemon juice, butter, and lemon zest until combined. Bring to a boil over medium-high heat. In a medium bowl, whisk together the eggs and egg yolks. Slowly pour half of the hot lemon into the egg mixture, whisking constantly. Pour the egg mixture into the saucepan; reduce the heat to medium-low. Cook, stirring constantly, until the mixture thickens and bubbles, 2 to 3 minutes. Remove from the heat and strain through a fine-mesh sieve into a container. Cover the surface directly with plastic wrap and chill until set before using, about 1 hour.

Classic Tiramisu

Gourmets may turn up their nose at tiramisu, the dessert that dominated restaurant menus throughout the late 1980s and '90s, but we all know we love it. And homemade tiramisu is heavenly—lighter and more flavorful than most. I will warn you, it's addictive, so be sure to make it when you plan to have company or else you'll lose track of how many passes you've made past the fridge, until you discover you've eaten the whole darn thing. No one's exercise regime can compensate for that! If you like a mellow tiramisu, use Marsala to brush the ladyfingers. The stronger flavors of brandy and rum are also wonderful, and you'll need less of them. Traditional Italian recipes use raw eggs to both enrich and lighten the dessert. If the possible presence of salmonella worries you, look for pasteurized eggs near the regular eggs in your supermarket. If possible, use real brewed espresso—just pick up three or four shots at your local coffeehouse and refrigerate it in an airtight container for up to 24 hours.

MAKES 16 SERVINGS.

⅓ C. brewed espresso (3 shots)

6 Tbs. Marsala or ¼ C. brandy or rum (divided)

2 pkgs. (3-oz.) soft ladyfingers (24 ladyfinger "halves" per pkg.)

2 (8-oz.) containers mascarpone cheese, at room temperature

¾ C. sugar (divided)

2 large eggs, separated

¼ tsp. salt

1 C. heavy whipping cream

¼ C. finely grated bittersweet chocolate or 2 Tbs. unsweetened cocoa powder for dusting

Combine the espresso and ¼ cup of the Marsala (or 2 tablespoons brandy or rum). Brush the espresso mixture over both sides of the ladyfingers; set the ladyfingers aside on a sheet of plastic wrap. (They get a bit sticky and soft.)

In a large bowl, whisk together the mascarpone cheese, ½ cup of the sugar, the egg yolks, and the remaining Marsala (or brandy/rum) until the mixture is smooth and free of lumps, about 45 seconds.

In a medium bowl, whip the egg whites with the salt until frothy. Gradually, a tablespoon at a time, beat in the remaining ¼ cup of sugar. Continue beating until stiff peaks form, about 3 minutes. In another chilled medium bowl, beat the heavy cream with a chilled whisk until stiff peaks form, 4 to 6 minutes; set aside.

Whisk one-third of the whipped cream into the mascarpone mixture to lighten. Fold in the remaining whipped cream and then the beaten egg whites with a silicone spatula until the mixture is just combined.

Line the bottom of a 9"-square pan (with sides at least 2½" high) with a single layer of the espresso-soaked ladyfingers. Top with half of the cream mixture, leveling by rapping the pan firmly on the counter. Top with a single layer of the remaining ladyfingers. Top with the remaining cream. The pan will be very full, mounded up toward the center.

Cover the top with plastic wrap. Chill until set, at least 1 hour, and preferably overnight for the flavors to meld. Sprinkle with the grated chocolate or dust with the cocoa powder using a fine-mesh sieve. Serve cold.

Tangy Panna Cotta with Fresh Berries

The name of a favorite Italian dessert, panna cotta, literally translates as "cooked cream." However, the cream is not really cooked, it's just set with gelatin. A good panna cotta should be firm enough to hold its shape when unmolded, yet melt instantly when it hits your tongue—a wonderful, cool, creamy sensation. It should never be rubbery. Panna cotta is a great summer dessert that's best appreciated with fresh, ripe berries, or cherries macerated with a bit of liqueur and sugar. I've used buttermilk here because the light, tangy flavor complements the heavy cream perfectly. You can make the dessert richer by using a bit of crème fraîche, sour cream, mascarpone, or full-fat yogurt in place of the some of buttermilk, or you can even use all low-fat yogurt in place of all the buttermilk.

MAKES 6 SERVINGS.

1½ C. heavy whipping cream (divided)

1 envelope unflavored gelatin (¼ oz.)

½ C. sugar

1¾ C. buttermilk

½ tsp. vanilla extract (optional)

1 C. sliced strawberries

1 C. blackberries

1 C. raspberries

Pour ¾ cup of the cream into a small saucepan. Sprinkle with the gelatin; let stand for 5 minutes for the gelatin to soften. Heat over low heat until the gelatin dissolves, 1 to 2 minutes, stirring occasionally. Stir in the sugar. Meanwhile, in a medium bowl, combine the remaining cream and the buttermilk. Pour the hot gelatin mixture into the cream and buttermilk, whisking constantly. Stir in the vanilla, if desired. Divide the mixture evenly among six 4-ounce ramekins. Refrigerate until cold and set, 4 to 6 hours.

To serve, using a small offset spatula or knife, loosen the panna cottas from the sides of the ramekins. Invert onto dessert plates, removing the ramekins. If the panna cotta doesn't budge, dip the bottom of the ramekin briefly into hot water. You may need to gently tap the ramekin on the plate to unmold it. Surround each panna cotta with about ½ cup berries.

Bittersweet Chocolate Mousse

This is a rich and creamy, take-no-prisoners kind of chocolate mousse. It's dense on the spoon but light on the tongue. If you like your mousse very light and airy and less rich, you can either beat a second egg white into the mousse or fold in a bit more whipped cream, but most chocoholics will like it as it is. Take note of the uncooked egg in this recipe—if the risk of salmonella bothers you, seek out pasteurized eggs. I have made cooked versions of chocolate mousse, but they lack the super-creamy texture I think a mousse should have. Chocolate mousse makes an elegant dessert served in parfait glasses with whipped cream and shaved chocolate (use a vegetable peeler). It's also a great filling for layer cakes and tarts with a cookie-crumb crust. You can double this recipe for a larger crowd.

MAKES 4 SERVINGS (A GENEROUS 2 CUPS)

¾ C. heavy whipping cream (divided)
1 (3.5-oz.) bar bittersweet chocolate, coarsely chopped
1 Tbs. brandy or rum
1 Tbs. Kahlúa (other coffee or even chocolate liqueurs are also fine)
½ tsp. vanilla extract
1 large egg, separated, at room temperature
Pinch of salt
2 Tbs. sugar

In a small saucepan, heat ¼ cup of the cream over medium-low heat. Stir in the chocolate, brandy or rum, Kahlúa, and vanilla until the mixture is smooth and the chocolate is completely melted. Remove from the heat. Whisk in the egg yolk; set aside.

In a clean, small bowl, beat the egg white and salt with a whisk until soft peaks form. Gradually, 1 tablespoon at a time, beat in the sugar. Continue beating until the whites are fluffy and smooth with no graininess and hold soft peaks when the whisk is lifted.

In another chilled, small bowl, beat the remaining cream with a whisk until soft peaks form.

Scrape the chocolate mixture into a large, shallow bowl. With a silicone spatula, gently fold in the beaten egg white until just incorporated. Fold in the whipped cream until just incorporated.

Divide the mousse evenly among 4 serving dishes and refrigerate until set, about 2 hours. Serve with additional whipped cream and garnish with chocolate shavings, if desired.

Gianduja Pots de Crème

I created this easy recipe a decade ago, and it's still a family favorite. A pot de crème is merely a custard baked in a water bath, usually in individual servings. Anything you make in individual servings will appear labor intensive and impressive to guests, and this quick and easy custard will definitely win you fans. I'm not normally a milk chocolate fan, but the combination of creamy hazelnut Nutella and milk chocolate may even surpass that other famous duo, peanut butter and chocolate.

MAKES 4 SERVINGS.

4 large egg yolks
1½ C. half-and-half

⅔ C. chocolate-hazelnut spread
6 oz. milk chocolate, finely chopped

Preheat the oven to 325°F. In a small bowl, whisk the egg yolks until smooth. In a small saucepan, combine the half-and-half and Nutella; heat, stirring occasionally, until smooth and melted. Increase the heat to medium-high. When the mixture begins to boil, pour approximately half of it into the egg yolks in a slow, steady stream, whisking constantly. Stir the egg mixture back into the saucepan and return to medium-low heat. Cook, stirring constantly, until the mixtures thickens and coats the back of a spoon. Do not boil. Remove the pan from the heat; stir in the chopped chocolate until melted and smooth. Strain the mixture into a heatproof measuring cup.

Arrange four 6-ounce ovenproof tea or coffee cups (or custard cups) in a shallow roasting pan. Divide the custard evenly among the cups. Place the roasting pan in the oven; pour enough hot water into the pan to come halfway up the sides of the cups. Bake for 20 to 25 minutes or until the custard is just a little wobbly in the center when the cups are jiggled. Do not overbake—the custards will set upon cooling.

Place a wire rack on a shelf in the refrigerator; arrange the cups on the rack. Refrigerate for 10 minutes, then cover loosely with plastic wrap. Chill completely, 4 to 6 hours, before serving.

This pie is an homage to my favorite childhood dessert, chocolate cream pie. I think I ordered a slice of chocolate cream pie every time we ate out at a restaurant as a family. Unfortunately, as I grew up my tastes changed, and the beloved pie of my youth seemed way too sweet. I had no choice but to design my own, and I think your family will love it, too. It's plenty sweet, despite the bittersweet chocolate, so even little ones will find it tasty. Don't forget the whipped cream topping—it's the perfect foil for all that chocolate and delectable crunchy pastry. The chocolate filling is just firm enough to slice, but it will melt as soon as it hits your tongue. If you want to turn this custard into a simple chocolate pudding, reduce the cornstarch to 2 tablespoons. The pudding may be served warm or cold.

MAKES 10 SERVINGS.

CHOCOLATE FILLING

2 C. milk

⅔ C. sugar

2 large eggs

2 large egg yolks

1 C. heavy whipping cream

¼ C. cornstarch

3 Tbs. unsweetened cocoa powder

Pinch of salt

2 (3.5-oz.) bars bittersweet chocolate, finely chopped

3 Tbs. unsalted butter, cut into pieces

1 tsp. vanilla extract

1 baked 9" Pie Pastry shell (see page 183)

GARNISH

1½ C. very cold heavy whipping cream

2 Tbs. sugar

For the chocolate filling, in a medium saucepan over medium-high heat, combine the milk and sugar. Bring to a boil, stirring occasionally to dissolve the sugar. Meanwhile, in a medium bowl, whisk together the eggs, egg yolks, cream, cornstarch, cocoa powder, and salt. Slowly pour half of the hot milk mixture into the eggs, whisking constantly. Pour the egg mixture into the pan, again whisking constantly. Cook over medium to low heat, whisking, until the mixture just comes to a boil, 4 to 6 minutes. Remove from the heat and stir in the chocolate, butter, and vanilla. Let stand for 2 minutes. Stir until the chocolate is completely melted. Strain the pudding through a fine-mesh sieve into the prepared pie shell. Cover the surface with plastic wrap and refrigerate until set, about 3 hours.

For the garnish, chill a metal bowl and whisk in the freezer or refrigerator. Beat the heavy whipping cream and sugar vigorously until stiff peaks form. Spread the whipped cream over the pie and serve.

Mocha-tini Pie

A friend once made me a chocolate martini that was so rich, creamy, and delicious that I drank two and wasn't hungry for dinner. Here I've turned those wonderful flavors into a fluffy cream pie. This is an adults-only dessert—there is quite a kick of alcohol. Choose good-quality liqueurs for the pie. I like the extra dark (and stronger flavor) of Kahlúa Especial for the coffee liqueur, and the wonderfully aromatic Lejay-Lagoute for the chocolate liqueur. If you want a more subtle flavor, omit the brandy and include Bailey's Irish Cream instead.

MAKES 8 SERVINGS.

COOKIE CRUST

1½ C. chocolate cookie crumbs*

¼ C. sugar

5 Tbs. unsalted butter, melted

*NOTE: Chocolate cookie crumbs: 1½ cup chocolate cookie crumbs is equal to three-quarters of a box of Nabisco's Famous Chocolate Wafers.

MOCHA FILLING

⅔ C. brewed strong coffee, cooled

1 envelope unflavored gelatin (¼ oz.)

2 large eggs, separated

½ C. sugar (divided)

2 tsp. instant espresso powder

⅛ tsp. salt

¼ C. coffee liqueur

2 Tbs. chocolate liqueur

2 Tbs. brandy

1¼ C. heavy whipping cream

Chocolate curls for garnish (optional)

Preheat the oven to 350°F.

For the crust, in a small bowl, stir together the cookie crumbs, sugar, and butter until well combined. Press into the bottom and up the sides of a 9" pie pan. Bake for 10 minutes; cool.

For the filling, combine the coffee and gelatin in a small saucepan over low heat. Whisk in the egg yolks, ⅓ cup of the sugar, the espresso powder, and the salt. Heat, stirring, until the gelatin dissolves and the mixture thickens. Do not boil. Remove from the heat. Stir in the liqueurs and brandy. Transfer the mixture to a metal bowl and chill in an ice-water bath, stirring occasionally, until the mixture mounds just bit.

In a clean bowl, beat the egg whites with a whisk until stiff; gradually, about a tablespoon at time, beat in the remaining sugar. Continue beating until stiff peaks form. Fold the whites into the chilled filling mixture. In a clean, very cold bowl, whip the cream with a whisk until soft peaks form. Fold into the mixture. Spoon the filling into the cookie crust. Chill for at least 4 hours or overnight. Garnish with chocolate curls, if desired.

Chocolate-Banana Cream Tart

If you cross a banana cream pie with a banana split, you'd get this tart. Complete with crunchy peanuts in the chocolate crumb crust and a fudgy glaze, this dessert is a sophisticated presentation of decidedly kid-friendly flavors. If you are a purist, you can omit the peanuts and put the banana cream filling in a graham crust, and even add toasted coconut as a garnish. Either way, you'll have a winner on your hands. This dessert needs no further garnish, but a little whipped cream never hurts.

MAKES 12 SERVINGS.

CHOCOLATE-PEANUT CRUMB CRUST

1½ C. chocolate cookie crumbs (see page 236)

¼ C. roasted peanuts, finely chopped

2 Tbs. sugar

6 Tbs. unsalted butter, melted

CREAM FILLING

1½ C. half-and-half

1 large egg

2 large egg yolks

6 Tbs. sugar

2½ Tbs. cornstarch

⅛ tsp. salt

1 Tbs. unsalted butter

1 Tbs. rum (optional)

¾ tsp. vanilla extract

FUDGY GANACHE DRIZZLE

½ C. heavy whipping cream

1 (3.5-oz.) bar bittersweet chocolate, finely chopped

ASSEMBLY

3 ripe-but-firm medium bananas

3 Tbs. lemon juice

2 Tbs. chopped roasted peanuts

Preheat the oven to 350°F. For the crust, in a medium bowl, stir together the cookie crumbs, peanuts, sugar, and butter until well combined. Press the mixture into the bottom and up the sides of an 11" x 7" tart pan with a removable bottom. Bake for 8 to 10 minutes or until the crust is set. Cool completely on a wire rack.

For the cream filling, in a medium saucepan, bring the half-and-half to a boil over high heat. In a medium bowl, whisk together the egg and egg yolks, sugar, cornstarch, and salt. Slowly pour the hot half-and-half into the egg mixture, whisking constantly. Pour the egg mixture into the saucepan; reduce the heat to medium-low. Cook, stirring constantly, until the mixture thickens and bubbles, 2 to 3 minutes. Remove from the heat and stir in the butter, rum if desired, and vanilla. Strain the filling through a fine-mesh sieve into the cooled tart shell, spreading evenly. Cover the surface directly with plastic wrap and chill for 3 hours.

For the ganache, bring the cream to a boil in small saucepan. Remove from the heat and stir in the chopped chocolate. Let stand for 1 minute; whisk until smooth. Cool to room temperature.

To assemble the tart, peel the bananas, and then slice crosswise at slight angle into ¼"-thick pieces. Toss the banana slices with the lemon juice. Starting at a corner of the pan, arrange a row of banana slices diagonally, letting the slices overlap a little. Arrange a second row of bananas below it; continue in this fashion until the entire surface of the tart is covered. Using a fork or a small spoon, drizzle the ganache across the tart. Sprinkle the top with the chopped peanuts. Serve with the remaining ganache, rewarming if needed.

Chocolate–Peanut Butter Cream Pie

This creamy pie with the crunchy chocolate crumb crust is my favorite combination of peanut butter and chocolate. It's such a cinch to make (the filling needs no baking) and is sure to become a favorite at your house. The molasses is a very interesting addition to this pie. Instead of tasting strong and assertive, it simply adds depth and makes the peanut flavor seem more, well, *peanutty*. Try it, you'll be surprised.

MAKES 10 SERVINGS.

1 C. creamy peanut butter (not natural style)
½ C. packed dark brown sugar
1 Tbs. molasses
1 tsp. vanilla extract

1 (8-oz.) pkg. cream cheese, at room temperature
1 C. heavy whipping cream
One 9" chocolate cookie crumb crust, baked (see page 236)

GARNISH

1½ C. very cold heavy whipping cream
2 Tbs. sugar

2 Tbs. chopped roasted peanuts or chocolate curls

In a large bowl, beat the peanut butter, brown sugar, molasses, and vanilla until smooth, about 1 minute. Beat in the cream cheese until the mixture is smooth, light, and fluffy, about 2 minutes.

In a clean, chilled bowl, whisk the 1 cup heavy cream until stiff peaks form, 3 to 4 minutes. Fold into the peanut butter mixture. Spoon the mixture into the prepared chocolate cookie crust. Refrigerate until firm, 3 to 4 hours.

For the garnish, chill a metal bowl and whisk in the freezer or refrigerator. Beat the cream and sugar vigorously until stiff peaks form, 4 to 6 minutes. Spread the whipped cream over the pie. For a fancier presentation, put the whipped cream in a pastry bag fitted with a large star tip and pipe rosettes of cream over the top of the pie. Sprinkle with the chopped peanuts or chocolate curls and serve.

Chocolate Ganache Tart with Caramel Sauce

This is the dessert to serve die-hard chocolate lovers and folks who don't care for sweet desserts. The pecan crust takes on an almost praline-like flavor as it bakes, and the deep amber caramel sauce cuts the rich chocolate with a hint of smokiness. Be sure to let the caramel really turn a rich, reddish amber before removing it from the heat, or it won't be flavorful enough. The heart of this dessert is the ganache, so splurge on excellent bar chocolate. Also note that bittersweet chocolates with a cocoa content above 70 percent may curdle the ganache: If this happens, simple stir in a small bit of sugar and/or cream until it smoothes out. Chocolate ganache, a simple combination of chocolate and cream, makes a rich, dreamy filling for all manner of tarts, so don't hesitate to get creative: Top the tart with sweetened whipped cream that has mascarpone cheese or even crème fraîche folded into it, or serve it in an all–graham cracker crust. You can add your favorite liqueur to the ganache, or espresso or a bit of reduced wine or port. I've even made a half-recipe of ganache, served it in a graham shell, and topped it with fresh raspberries.

MAKES 16 SERVINGS.

PECAN-GRAHAM CRUST

1¼ C. graham cracker crumbs
1¼ C. finely chopped pecans
½ C. sugar

¼ tsp. salt
6 Tbs. unsalted butter, melted

GANACHE FILLING

¾ C plus 2 Tbs. heavy whipping cream

3 (3.5-oz) bars bittersweet chocolate, finely chopped

Caramel Sauce (page 152)

For the crust, preheat the oven to 350°F. In a medium bowl, stir together the graham cracker crumbs, pecans, sugar, salt, and butter until well combined. Press the crumb mixture into the bottom and up the sides of a 9½"-fluted removable-bottom tart pan. Bake for 11 to 12 minutes or until fragrant and lightly browned. Cool in the pan on a wire rack.

Meanwhile, for the ganache, in a large, heavy saucepan, bring the cream to a boil over medium-high heat. Remove from the heat and add the chocolate. Let stand for 1 minute. Stir until smooth and the chocolate is completely melted. Pour the ganache into the baked crust. Refrigerate overnight or until set, at least 4 hours.

Serve the tart cool but not cold. (Allow least 15 minutes to warm up out of the refrigerator.) Serve with warm Caramel Sauce, reheating if necessary.

Creamy White Chocolate–Cointreau Tartlettes

These are essentially mini orange-flavored cheesecakes masquerading as a fancier dessert. Though using individual tart pans makes for an elegant presentation, you can use two 9½" tart shells instead. I love the contrast of the almond-gingersnap crust against the orange-scented filling, but you can use graham crackers if gingersnaps don't appeal to you. The cranberry sauce is optional—a great way of dressing up the dessert for autumn holidays. The rest of the year, I serve the cheese tarts plain or with fresh berries on the side.

MAKES 8 SERVINGS.

GINGERSNAP CRUSTS

1 (12 oz.) box gingersnap cookies, finely crushed

1¼ C. toasted sliced almonds, ground in a rotary cheese grater

⅓ C. sugar

10 Tbs. unsalted butter, melted

WHITE CHOCOLATE CHEESE FILLING

1 lb. cream cheese, at room temperature

¾ C. sugar

2 Tbs. all-purpose flour

2 large eggs, at room temperature

2 large egg yolks, at room temperature

2 (3.5-oz.) bars Lindt or Rainforest white chocolate, melted

½ C. heavy whipping cream, at room temperature

2 Tbs. Cointreau or other orange liqueur

1 tsp. orange extract

CRANBERRY SAUCE

1½ C. fresh or thawed frozen cranberries

2 C. water

1 C. sugar

½ tsp. orange extract

Preheat the oven to 350°F. For the gingersnap crusts, in a large bowl, stir together the gingersnaps, almonds, sugar, and butter until well combined. Divide the mixture evenly among eight 4" x 1" fluted removable-bottom pans. Press the crumbs into the bottom and up the sides of the pans. Chill until needed.

For the white chocolate–cheese filling, in a large bowl, beat the cream cheese until light and fluffy. Add the sugar and flour and continue beating until the mixture is smooth and even fluffier, 2 to 3 minutes. One at a time, beat in the eggs and then the egg yolks until each is incorporated. Stir in the melted white chocolate, cream, Cointreau, and orange extract until the batter is smooth.

Place the prepared tartlet pans on a baking sheet. Divide the filling among the tarts, filling to just under ⅛" from the top. Bake (on the baking sheet) for 30 to 35 minutes or until the filling is set and slightly puffed. Cool on a wire rack until just warm; remove from the pans and cool completely.

Meanwhile, to make the cranberry sauce, bring the cranberries, water, and sugar to a boil in a medium saucepan over medium-high heat. Boil, stirring occasionally, until the mixture is reduced by about a third, 10 to 12 minutes. Press through a fine-mesh sieve and return to the saucepan. Bring to a boil once again and skim off any foam. Remove from the heat and stir in the orange extract.

Place each tart on an individual serving plate. Spoon some cranberry sauce to one side and serve.

Lime-Coconut-Macadamia Tart

Tart and tangy like a lime pie should be, this dessert is also airy and light like a mousse, delightful against the chewy-crisp macaroon-like crust. You could achieve the same effect by omitting the tart crust and serving the mousse with cookies. (I suggest the Coconut-Almond Lace Tuiles (page 114) or the Double Ginger Butter Crisps (page 104). The mousse itself is a hybrid recipe: sort of a lime curd turned into a ganache, then lightened with whipped cream into a mousse. It's important that the lime mixture be just barely warm when the cream is folded in, or the air will melt out of the cream and flatten the mousse. A wire whisk with flexible, wide-spaced tines makes fast and efficient work out of the folding.

MAKES 12 SERVINGS.

MACADAMIA-COCONUT CRUST

1½ C. whole blanched macadamia nuts, finely chopped

1 C. lightly packed sweetened flaked coconut, finely chopped

½ C. graham cracker crumbs

2 Tbs. packed light brown sugar

¼ cup unsalted butter, melted

LIME-COCONUT FILLING

½ C. lime juice

⅓ C. sugar

1 large egg

2 large egg yolks

1 tsp. grated lime zest

1 (3.5-oz.) bar Lindt Excellence White Coconut chocolate or plain Lindt white chocolate, finely chopped

1 C. heavy whipping cream

GARNISH

½ C. heavy whipping cream

2 Tbs. powdered sugar

2 Tbs. minced crystallized ginger

Preheat the oven to 350°F. For the crust, in a medium bowl, stir together the macadamia nuts, coconut, graham cracker crumbs, brown sugar, and butter until well combined. Press the mixture into the bottom and up the sides of an 11" x 7" fluted tart pan with a removable bottom. Bake for 18 to 20 minutes or until the crust is set. Cool completely on a wire rack.

For the filling, in a small metal bowl set over a pan of simmering water, whisk together the lime juice, sugar, egg, egg yolks, and lime zest. Cook, whisking constantly, until the mixture visibly thickens (when the handle of a wooden spoon is drawn through the mixture, you will be able to see the bottom of the bowl briefly before the filling oozes back together). Remove from the heat and stir in the white chocolate until melted and smooth. Cool on the counter for 5 to 7 minutes, until barely warm. Meanwhile, in medium chilled bowl, whip the cream with a whisk until stiff peaks form. Whisk one-third of the whipped cream into the lime mixture until smooth. Gently fold in the remaining whipped cream. Spoon the mixture into the prepared crust. Chill until set, 1 to 2 hours.

For the garnish, in a medium chilled metal bowl, whip the cream and powdered sugar until stiff peaks form. Transfer the whipped cream to a pastry bag fitted with a star tip. Pipe rosettes all around the edge of the tart. Garnish each rosette with a bit of crystallized ginger.

Butterscotch-Walnut Tart

Paired with the slightly bitter flavor of walnuts, this is a very grown-up version of the butterscotch pudding-from-a-box of my childhood. The secret is to cook the butterscotch until it starts to darken and caramelize around the edges, which gives it considerable depth and character. Stirring in a mere tablespoon of rum or brandy will heighten the flavors nicely. This makes a thin layer of butterscotch, but a little goes a long way. Top the tart with whipped cream and more toasted walnuts. If you prefer the praline flavor of toasted pecans, use them in place of the walnuts.

MAKES 12 SERVINGS.

WALNUT CRUST

1 C. graham cracker crumbs

½ C. very finely chopped walnuts

¼ C. unsalted butter, melted

3 Tbs. packed light brown sugar

BUTTERSCOTCH FILLING

3 Tbs. unsalted butter

2 Tbs. light corn syrup

¾ C. packed light brown sugar

1⅓ C. milk

¼ tsp. salt

2 large egg yolks

2 Tbs. cornstarch

1 Tbs. brandy or rum

½ tsp. vanilla extract

TOPPING

¾ C. heavy whipping cream

⅓ C. toasted chopped walnuts

Preheat the oven to 350°F. For the crust, in a medium bowl, stir together the graham cracker crumbs, walnuts, butter, and brown sugar until well combined. Press the mixture into the bottom and up the sides of an 11" x 7" fluted tart pan with a removable bottom. Bake for 10 to 11 minutes or until the crust is set. Cool completely on a wire rack.

For the filling, in a small, heavy pan, melt the butter with the corn syrup over medium-high heat. Stir in the brown sugar and cook, stirring occasionally, for 5 to 6 minutes. (The mixture will darken at the edges and become fragrant as it caramelizes; a candy thermometer will register 260°F. when inserted into the center of the liquid.) Remove the pan from the heat, but keep in a warm spot.

Meanwhile, in a medium saucepan, whisk together the milk and salt until smooth. Bring to a boil over medium-high heat. Whisk the egg yolks and the cornstarch together in a small bowl until smooth. Slowly pour the hot milk mixture into the yolks, whisking constantly. Pour the egg mixture into the pan set over medium-low heat. Cook, stirring constantly, until the mixture thickens and bubbles, 2 to 3 minutes. Remove from the heat and stir in the butterscotch mixture, brandy or rum, and vanilla. Strain the filling through a fine-mesh sieve into the cooled tart shell, spreading evenly. Cover the surface with plastic wrap and chill for 3 hours.

For the topping, in a medium chilled metal bowl, whip the cream with a whisk until stiff peaks form. Place the whipped cream in a pastry bag fitted with a star tip and pipe a decorative lattice over the tart. (Alternately, gently spread the whipped cream over the top of the tart with an offset spatula.) Sprinkle with the walnuts.

Lemon Pudding Cake

Cake on top and custard on the bottom, pudding cake is two desserts in one. Made by stirring whipped egg whites into a thin batter, pudding cake is essentially a soufflé with too much liquid. And nothing could be easier—overbeating the egg whites is made nigh impossible by the addition of sugar in the early stage of beating, which both stabilizes and buffers the egg foam. Pudding cake can be served warm, about 30 minutes out of the oven, but I highly recommend delaying gratification until it is thoroughly chilled. Served cold, the flavors intensify and the two layers are more distinct. These individual-serving pudding cakes have the virtue of cooling down faster, hence making it to the table sooner—not to mention offering a fancier presentation.

MAKES 6 SERVINGS.

¼ C. unsalted butter, melted
1 C. sugar (divided)
3 large eggs, separated, at room
    temperature
¼ C. all-purpose flour

¼ tsp. plus ⅛ tsp. salt
1¼ C. milk, at room temperature
⅓ C. lemon juice, at room
    temperature
Grated zest of 1 large lemon

Preheat the oven to 350°F. Butter eight 6-ounce ceramic ovenproof ramekins; set aside. In a large bowl, whisk together the butter, ⅔ cup of the sugar, and the egg yolks until smooth and fluffy, about 1 minute. Add the flour and salt to the bowl; slowly drizzle in the milk, whisking constantly, until the mixture is smooth. Whisk in the lemon juice. The mixture will be thin.

Beat the egg whites in a clean bowl with a large balloon whisk until soft peaks form. Gradually, a few teaspoons at a time, beat in the remaining sugar. Continue beating until the sugar is completely dissolved (no grittiness) and medium-stiff peaks form when you pull the whisk away.

Scrape the egg whites into the bowl with the egg yolk mixture. Sprinkle the zest on top. With the whisk, quickly but gently fold the egg whites into the batter. Divide the mixture evenly among the ramekins—since the cakes do not really rise, you can fill them to within ⅛" of the top. Place the ramekins in a roasting pan. Pour warm water into the pan, reaching halfway up the sides of the ramekins. Bake for 25 minutes, until the tops are golden and spring back when touched. As with soufflés, there is no absolute way to judge doneness, so be sure to set a timer. Remove the custards from the hot water bath and place them over a wire rack to cool. Cool for 30 minutes to set completely—pudding cakes will curdle and separate if stirred while hot. Serve just warm, or, better yet, refrigerate until completely chilled. Pudding cakes are excellent served with a dollop of whipped cream.

Anytime Bread Pudding

This is called "anytime" pudding because I actually don't make bread pudding for dessert; I eat it at breakfast or as an afternoon snack. It reminds me of French toast. But since it's technically a dessert, and I knew readers would never find it if I put it with the breakfast foods, it's here in the custard chapter, where it arguably belongs. The flavors are dark rum and raisins, a classic bread pudding pairing, but I've also included a Sour Cherry–Amaretto variation. Bread pudding is one of those desserts best made a day ahead—you'll find that the flavor and texture improve with time. Often I am so lazy that I'll let the bread cubes soak up the custard overnight in the refrigerator before baking the next day—that also makes a wonderfully tender bread pudding. Any stale bread will work in this recipe, even day-old cinnamon bread.

MAKES 9 SERVINGS.

2 C. milk

½ cup raisins

1½ C. heavy whipping cream

1 C. sugar

¼ C. dark rum

2 tsp. vanilla extract

Pinch of freshly grated nutmeg

4 large eggs

1 (1-lb.) artisan bread loaf, preferably sourdough, cut into 1" squares (about 6 C.)

In a medium saucepan, heat the milk with the raisins over medium heat until the milk is very warm but not boiling. Pour into a large bowl and whisk in the cream, sugar, rum, vanilla, and nutmeg. Whisk in the eggs until smooth. Stir in the bread chunks, making sure that all the pieces are submerged. Let stand at room temperature, covered, stirring occasionally, until most of the liquid is absorbed, 45 minutes to 1 hour. (Alternately, you may place the bread-custard mixture into the prepared baking dish, cover with plastic wrap, place a plate on top of the plastic wrap, weight down with a few cans, and refrigerate overnight. Allow to warm up for 30 minutes at room temperature before baking.)

Preheat the oven to 325°F. Butter a 9"-square baking dish. Spoon the bread mixture into the baking dish and cover with a sheet of buttered aluminum foil. Set the baking dish in a shallow roasting pan. Place the roasting pan in the oven; pour enough hot water into the pan to come halfway up the side of the baking dish. Bake for 30 minutes or until the center is a little wobbly in the center when jiggled. Remove the foil and bake for 20 minutes more. Do not overbake—bread pudding will set upon cooling. Cool for 15 minutes on a wire rack. Serve warm or cold.

→ **SOUR CHERRY–AMARETTO BREAD PUDDING:** Substitute ½ cup sour dried cherries for the raisins, reduce the vanilla extract to 1½ teaspoons, add ½ teaspoon almond extract, and substitute ¼ cup amaretto for the dark rum.

index